Collins

a year of nature walks and games

52 things to see and do

Becky Goddard-Hill & Catherine Hughes

Published by Collins
An imprint of HarperCollins Publishers
Westerhill Road, Bishopbriggs, Glasgow G64 2QT
www.harpercollins.co.uk

HarperCollins Publishers
Macken House,
39/40 Mayor Street Upper,
Dublin 1, D01 C9W8, Ireland

The contents of this publication are believed correct at the time of printing. Every care has been taken in
the preparation of this book. However, the publisher accepts no responsibility whatsoever for any loss,
damage, injury or inconvenience sustained or caused as a result of using this book. The user is advised to
take appropriate care when taking part in any of the activities included herein.

A catalogue record for this book is available from the British Library

ISBN 978-0-00-859496-1

10 9 8 7 6 5 4 3 2 1

Printed in the UAE

If you would like to comment on any aspect of this book, please contact us at the above address or online.

This book is produced from independently certified FSC™ paper
to ensure responsible forest management.

For more information visit: www.harpercollins.co.uk/green

Huge thanks to Michelle I'Anson, Lauren Murray, Hilary Stein, Kevin Robbins and Gordon MacGilp for the vision and creativity to bring this nature book to life.

Becky: To Frankie and Annalise, may you always skim stones, climb trees and feel small when you stand beside the ocean.

I love you with all my heart.

Catherine: For my lovely mum and dad - thank you for letting me keep snails as pets, for putting up with mud pies in the lawn, and for helping me learn to love nature.

Author of *Create Your Own Happy*, *Create Your Own Calm* and *Create Your Own Kindness*, Becky Goddard-Hill is a children's therapist and former social worker with a specialism in child development. She is also a professionally qualified life coach and member of the National Council of Psychotherapists. She is an enthusiastic believer in the power of creativity and nature to support children's emotional health and well-being.

Catherine Hughes has turned a lifelong passion for nature and gardening into a thriving career as a home and garden writer and blogger. Catherine's blog Growing Family is a Vuelio top 10 gardening blog. She is passionate about encouraging children to explore and enjoy nature, and writes regularly on nature activities, children's gardening and crafts.

Becky and Catherine are also the authors of *A Year of Nature Craft and Play*, a fun activity book that follows the seasons with nature-themed crafts and projects.

Contents

Autumn

Winter

Index

Introduction

Hello and welcome to this jam-packed book of nature walks and games!

Nature is amazing, interesting, ever changing, and just outside your door no matter where you live. From clouds to spider's webs, frosty walls to sunsets, you can't help but be impressed by nature.

You also never need to wait till summer or a 'nice day' either, because nature has treasure and adventures all year round. In fact, our book follows the seasons, so you have something to do outside in nature every single week of the year.

Perhaps when someone has suggested a walk to you in the past, you might have thought, 'Oh no, how boring,' – but once you have looked through this book you will know that a walk in nature can be the most awesome activity ever. Maybe you will go geocaching, learn survival skills, collect fallen nature treasures, pick fruit, or hide stones on your walk. This book has SO many ideas.

Games ideas are plentiful too: camping games and naming games, park games and even treasure-seeking games to keep you, your friends and your family always entertained when you head outside.

As well as walk ideas and fun games, you will also find some nature-based bakes, crafts and science activities within this book.

Nature is the most precious and beautiful, fascinating and fabulous part of our world. We hope this book helps you to see that and encourages you to take care of it, protect it and enjoy it.

Just remember the rules of the countryside code on the next page.

The countryside code

Respect everyone

- Be considerate to those living in, working in and enjoying the countryside.

- Leave gates and property as you find them.

- Do not block access to gateways or driveways when parking.

- Be nice, say hello, share the space.

- Follow local signs and keep to marked paths unless wider access is available.

Protect the environment

- Take your litter home – leave no trace of your visit.

- Do not light fires and only have BBQs where signs say you can.

- Always keep dogs under control and in sight.

- Bag and bin dog poo – any public waste bin will do.

- Care for nature – do not cause damage or disturbance, and only pick fallen flowers or flowers from your own garden or with permission.

Enjoy the outdoors

- Check your route and local conditions.

- Plan your adventure – know what to expect and what you can do.

- Enjoy your visit, have fun, make a memory.

Pass it on

We would love it if you could help us spread the word about how amazing and fun nature can be.

If you try an activity in the book and enjoy it, please pass it on to a friend who you think might enjoy it too.

If you make something beautiful from nature and think it might make someone smile, please pass it on.

And if you complete all the activities in this book, rather than leave it on a shelf, please pass it on!

Wishing you happy and creative nature-filled days.

Love Becky & Catherine

Spring

Nature is absolutely bursting with life in spring. Plants and trees are waking up, with new leaves and beautiful flowers for us to enjoy. Wildlife is busy gathering food, building nests and looking after babies. The sun starts to feel warmer, and if there's a spring shower you might be lucky enough to see a rainbow.

As the days get longer and the weather warms up, it's time to make the most of all that nature has to offer.

We've got lots of great ways to have fun on a spring walk, from memory and photography challenges to making nature postcards and chasing the sunset.

You can have a go at foraging, explore sounds and leaf science, learn about water wildlife and enjoy stick games from around the world. Perhaps you'd like to look after your local area with some beautiful nature art, or get involved with some community gardening?

Nature in springtime is an exciting place to be – let's join the celebration!

1 | Seek out the sunset

Watching the sun go down is incredible. In spring, sunset happens early enough for you to easily observe it, and there's no better way to enjoy the amazing views than on an evening walk.

The sun rises in the east and sets in the west, so use a compass or map to work out which direction you need to go in. During spring, the sun sets slightly later each day, so it's a good idea to use the internet to find out the sunset time. You then need to walk to a place where you will get a clear view to the west, so you can see the sun going down.

A hilltop or empty field is a good place, as you'll get a great view of the sunset with nothing to block it. By a river or canal works well too as you get the most gorgeous reflections, and a west-facing beach is perfect.

You could take with you:

- A picnic, and blanket – the sun takes a while to set, and it is lovely to watch it all

- A camera

- Your sketchbook and paints/crayons/pens to capture the colours you see

Back at home...

You might be so awed and inspired by what you have seen that you'll want to develop your sketch, print out your photos or share them. Maybe you want to make a collage of a sunset or write a poem. Nature can inspire great art!

No two sunsets are the same...

Seeing the sunset at different times of the year and from a variety of different places means this is an experience that always brings something new.

Where might you go to see it next?

The power of awe...

Scientists have found that being awed by nature helps people feel kinder towards each other, less worried about small things, and more peaceful.

Try it and see if a sunset on a tricky day can make you feel better!

2 | Perfect pairs scavenger hunt

There is so much to see in spring, and a scavenger hunt is a great way to get exploring. This one is a little different, though, and will really make you think!

You will need

- 2 envelopes, one labelled '1' and the other '2'
- 30 little slips of paper

Write the following words onto the slips of paper, one word per slip:

Black	Brown	Green
Red	Blue	Yellow
Pink	White	Rough
Smooth	Shiny	Prickly
Soft	Hard	Squishy

Then fold each piece of paper in half and put them all in envelope 1.

Now write these words on the remaining slips of paper:

Small	Big	Heavy
Light	Still	Moving
Quiet	Noisy	Patterned
Plain	Circle	Square
High	Low	Wet

And put these slips of paper, folded up, into envelope 2.

How to play

Head out on your walk. Your scavenger hunt begins when you draw a slip of paper from each envelope and set off to find something that matches the two-word description.

Big + White = **Swan**

Or

Wet + Brown = **Mud**

12

The rules

You can do this scavenger hunt on your own or as a competition to see who finds something that matches the description first. You can even do it as a race against the clock, seeing how many of the pairs you can discover in a set amount of time.

You decide how you want to play, and change the rules any time you like – you might even want to make some extra words!

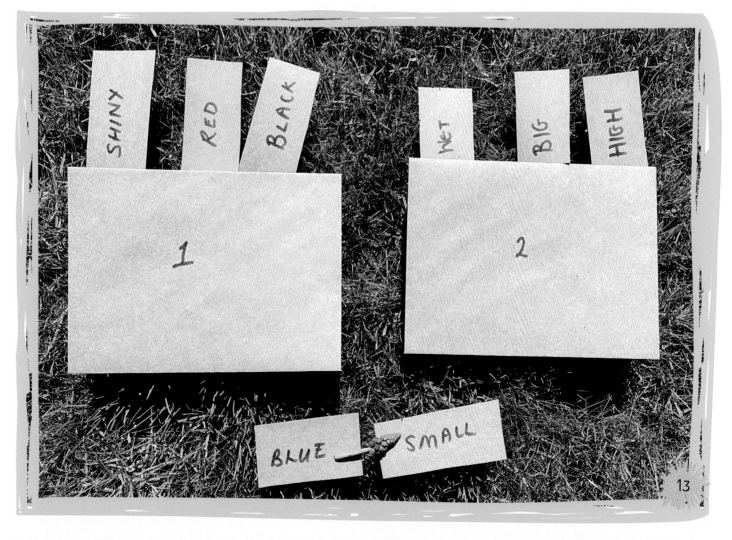

3 | A trip down memory lane

Let's take a walk down memory lane and make a tour of places that hold special memories for you.

Maybe you want to walk by where your best friend used to live, that tree you climbed when you were little, or that swing you played on for hours and hours?

Reliving old memories can make you feel warm and happy.

Preparation

Ask your grown-up to help you plan a route that takes in important places. They might even come up with a few that you haven't considered!

Next, make a plan detailing where you want to go. Consider how long it will take and how you will get around.

Can you walk there, or might you need to hop on your bike or a bus?

You will need

- A plan of where you want to visit and how to get there (perhaps you could make a map)

- A pocket notebook and pen

- A camera

Things to think about on your walk

As you revisit these special places, think about and chat about your memories. You might want to ask your grown-up what they remember too (after all, you might not remember your first day at nursery!).

You may want to make some brief notes in your notebook so you can write these memories up later, and snap some photos to record your special places.

Making a memory book

Your map, photos, notes and the things you have remembered can all go towards making a 'My Memories' book.

When you are older it is brilliant to look back on your life and think about all the things you have done. And it is super helpful to have your memories gathered all together so you don't forget anything.

Using the photos and details from your walk, you can put together a memory book that might show where you were born and first lived, what your hobbies were, where you went to school, where you played outside, and so on. It might take some time and a few trips down memory lane to piece everything together, but you will be so glad you did it.

A simple scrapbook or large, unlined journal are perfect for this (and if you keep adding to it over the years you may end up with a few volumes!).

Imagine, one day you could be showing your grandchildren a history of all your adventures from your special memory book.

Variations

You could ask your grandparents or parents to take you on a memory walk from their past too. It would be fascinating to see where they grew up, played and went to school. This might even involve a longer journey, and you would find out so much about their lives in the process.

On the Park.....

← Our favourite picnic spot

The best swing ever →

Grandma's memory bench

4 Stick games from around the world

Sticks are the most amazing things when it comes to playing outdoors. With just a simple stick, you can create all sorts of games and have hours of fun.

Sticks are easy to find in most countries, so as you can probably imagine, stick games are played by children all over the world.

Here are some popular stick games from around the world for you to try with your friends. You can play them in pairs or in teams.

South Africa – Drie Stokkies (Three Sticks)

How to play

1. Find three sticks, each 1 to 1.5 metres long.

2. Place the sticks parallel to each other on the ground. Make sure there is a space of about 0.5 to 1 metre between each stick (depending on the size of the children playing).

3. Players or teams stand at opposite sides of the sticks.

4. The first player runs up to the sticks, then takes one step in the space between the first and second sticks, one step between the second and third sticks, and after that jumps as far as they can over the third stick.

5. The third stick that the player jumped over is moved to where the player landed.

6. The other player/team is next, doing the same thing from the other side of the sticks. Again, the third stick they jumped over is moved to where they landed.

7. The middle stick stays where it is, while the sticks on either side move further out as more players jump.

8. If a player doesn't make it over the third stick with their jump, they are out and the stick stays where it is.

9. The winner is the last person in, who will have jumped the furthest.

China - Knocking the Stick

How to play

1. Draw two lines on the ground, about 2.5 metres apart.

2. Place a stick on one of the lines.

3. Each player or team takes it in turns to stand behind the other line and throw a stick, aiming it at the stick on the line. The aim is to knock the stick off the line.

4. The winner is the first player to knock the stick off the line.

Europe - Mikado

How to play

1. Find a selection of sticks. Ideally, one should look different from the rest – this is the 'special stick'.

2. One player holds all the sticks in one hand, places the bottom end of the bundle on the ground, and lets go. The sticks should fall to the ground in a jumble.

3. Each player then takes it in turns to try to remove a stick without touching or moving any of the other sticks. They can use their hands, or the special stick if they already have it.

4. If the player successfully removes a stick, they keep it and try to remove another one. When they touch or move any of the other sticks, they are out and the next player takes a turn.

5. Play continues until all the sticks have been removed.

6. The winner is the player with the most sticks.

7. You can make this game harder by using sticks that all look different, and giving each type a score. The winner is the player with the highest score from all the sticks they have removed.

Bolivia – La Palma

How to play

1. Find a short stick and some stones (if you prefer, you can use tennis balls instead of stones).

2. Use the stick to draw six parallel lines in the ground, each about 1 metre apart.

3. Push the stick into the ground about 1 metre beyond the last line.

4. Players take it in turns to stand on the first line and throw a stone. The aim is to hit the stick that is in the ground.

5. If the player misses, the next player takes a turn. If they hit the stick, they move up to the second line and throw again.

6. The winner is the first player to hit the stick while standing on each of the six lines.

Brazil - Hit the Coin

How to play

1. Find a straight stick with a flat end.

2. Push the stick into the ground, with the flat end sticking up.

3. Use another stick or a stone to draw a circle around the stick, about 30 cm out from it.

4. Place a coin on the flat end of the stick.

5. Each player takes it in turns to throw a coin. The aim is to knock the coin off the top of the stick so that it lands outside the circle.

6. If the player knocks the coin off and it lands outside the circle, they get one point and have another go. If the coin falls inside the circle or they miss, the next player takes a turn.

7. The player who has the most points at the end of the game is the winner.

8. To make things harder, you can stand further back from the stick when you throw your coin. To make things easier, you can stand closer or make the circle smaller.

Life is more fun if you play games.
Roald Dahl

5 | Community gardening

Gardening is a great hobby. It helps to keep you healthy and it's a brilliant way to relax and connect with nature.

Gardening can also bring people together in your local community. Gardening with your friends and neighbours is lots of fun, and can help to make your local area more nature-friendly.

Find out about community gardening near you

There might be a community garden close to where you live. These are gardens that are looked after by local residents, and you can join in with the gardening projects they are working on. To find out if you have a community garden near you, you could contact your local council, ask local gardening groups, or use the finder tool at www.farmgarden.org.uk.

Seed or Plant Swap

If you've grown more plants than you need, or have a few seeds leftover, why not share them with your friends or neighbours? They might have some plants or seeds to spare that they could give you in return.

A seed or plant swap helps to reduce waste, and can also save people money. You will end up with some lovely new seeds and plants for your own gardening projects too.

Sunflower Competition

How about organising a fun gardening competition for your school or street?

Sunflowers are easy to grow from seed, and because they are tall plants they're perfect for a height competition. Spring is the best time to plant sunflower seeds, and when they flower in summer you can take your measurements. The winner is the person with the tallest plant.

Plant Stall for Charity

You could grow some plants and sell them to raise money for charity. You could have a stall at your school fair, or at the local community garden, fete or market.

Sow wildflowers in neglected places

Is there a bare patch of public land close to where you live? You could scatter some wildflower seeds on the earth to turn it into a place that everyone can enjoy. When the seeds grow, they will make the area look beautiful and provide wildlife with food and shelter.

Spring and autumn are great times of year to sow seeds. Do make sure you only scatter seeds on public land though, and avoid private property.

6 | Capture the colour

Nature starts to get really colourful in spring. Flowers, leaves and trees all burst into life, insects and birds are out and about, and spring sunshine makes all the colours look lovely and bright.

This game is about noticing and recording all the amazing colour that nature is providing at this time of year. It's perfect for playing on a walk or a trip to the park.

You will need

- Some paper or a notebook

- A pencil

- A smartphone or camera (optional)

- Your observational skills

How to play

- Choose a colour.

- Start looking around for things you can see in nature that are the same colour. Some colours will be easier to find than others!

- You don't have to collect anything.

Instead, you can either try to remember all the items you spot, use your pencil and paper to make a list of them, or take a photo with a smartphone or camera.

- To make things more tricky, you could set a time limit for each colour.

- If you haven't already made a list, write down all the items you found after you've finished searching for your chosen colour.

- Repeat with other colours until you're ready to finish the game.

• Count up the number of items on each colour list, then add all the totals together to get your score.

• If you're playing this game in teams, the winner is the team with the highest score at the end of the game. You could also have a separate contest for each colour.

• If you're playing on your own, you might like to repeat the game next time you go out for a walk, to see if you can beat either your total score or your score for each colour.

Nature always wears the colours of the spirit.
Ralph Waldo Emerson

7 | Amazing leaf science

After months of bare branches, the leaves are back!

It's time to celebrate this leafy loveliness when you go for a walk or play outside.

You could take some time to notice all the shades of green, listen to the sound of leaves fluttering in the breeze, run your fingers gently through some leaves on a branch, or watch the patterns made by sunlight shining through the trees.

You can also use leaves in these amazing leaf experiments to understand how plants breathe and drink.

How do plants breathe?

You need sunshine for this experiment, so make sure you do it on a sunny day.

> I've seen a jillion miracles. They're all around. Every green leaf is a miracle.
> Jimmy Dean

You will need

- A large, fresh leaf from a plant or a tree
- A see-through bowl filled with lukewarm water
- A small stone
- A magnifying glass (optional)

What to do

1. Put the leaf in the bowl of water.

2. Place the stone on top of the leaf so that the leaf stays under the water. If this doesn't work, you may need to use a larger, heavier stone.

3. Put the bowl outside in the sunshine and leave it there for a few hours.

4. Come back regularly and take a look at the leaf. You should be able to see little bubbles on the leaf or on the bowl. The leaf is breathing out!

What's going on?

Trees and plants use a process called *photosynthesis* to make their food. Their leaves use energy from the sun to convert carbon dioxide and water into oxygen and sugar. As part of this process, the leaves release oxygen into the air.

To explain this another way, leaves breathe in carbon dioxide, and breathe out oxygen – and we all need oxygen to survive. This is one of the reasons why trees and plants are such an important part of nature and life on our planet.

Photosynthesis is happening in the leaf in the bowl. The oxygen gas is trapped in the water, and you can see it as little bubbles.

What would happen if the leaf wasn't in water?

How do plants drink?

This experiment works really well if you use celery or large lettuce leaves. You could grow your own leaves or buy them.

Once you've set the experiment up, it can take a few hours for you to see results – so be patient!

You will need

- Celery stalks with leaves still attached, or pale, firm lettuce leaves

- A see-through glass or jar

- Some food colouring

- A spoon and knife

- A magnifying glass (optional)

What to do

1. Pour water into your glass or jar until it's about half full.

2. Add a few drops of food colouring to the water and give it a stir with the spoon. For the best results, make the colour nice and strong.

3. Ask a grown-up to trim a little bit off the end of the celery stalk or leaf.

4. Place the stalk or leaf into the coloured water. Make sure the trimmed end is fully immersed.

5. Wait! Keep checking your stalk or leaf to see what happens to it. You should be able to see the leaf's veins changing colour as they fill with the coloured water. The leaf is drinking!

What's going on?

Plants and trees use something called *transpiration* to move water around. As water evaporates from their leaves, more water is pulled up through their stems to keep the leaves hydrated.

By colouring the water, you can see this process in action, as the stalk or leaf replaces the water that it lost through evaporation. Do some colours work better than others? Why do you think this is?

8 | The A-Z walk

Why not take an alphabet walk today and look for the shapes of all the letters of the alphabet in the things that you see around you as you walk? You could take a camera and get a photograph for each letter from A to Z.

Searching for the alphabet encourages you to look really closely at the world around you and the shapes that it forms.

Preparation
- Plan where you want to go and who might join you on your walk.

- If you need permission or a lesson in using the camera, it is best to do this before you set off, so do ask your grown-up.

- Don't forget to charge your camera battery beforehand!

You will need

- A camera or camera phone

- A list of all the letters from A to Z

- A pen

Things to think about on your walk
You probably won't find your letters in alphabetical order, so tick them off on your A-Z list as you find them, to help you keep track of those you have photographed.

Sometimes you might see letters forming naturally. Perhaps a stick that looks like a Y or an L. A round stone could be O. Perhaps a T could be formed where a path splits in two directions?

For other letters, you might want to create them yourself from bits of fallen nature such as petals or leaves, or from branches or pebbles.

Make a photo collage
After your adventure, you could use a photo editing app to make a collage of your photos in alphabetical order and print it out.

Perhaps you could use the letters that you have photographed to spell out your name, and edit them to create a picture you can print? You might even want to frame it and display it in your room. Or you could make one as a present for somebody.

There is another alphabet, whispering from every leaf, singing from every river, shimmering from every sky.
Dejan Stojanovic

29

9 | Wonderful water wildlife

Here's an amazing fact: freshwater habitats make up only around 3 per cent of the water on our planet, but they are home to over 100,000 different species of living thing!

Rivers, lakes, ponds and streams are all examples of freshwater habitats. The water is very low in salt (unlike the sea), and they are bursting with life if you know where to look.

Spring is a good time to explore water wildlife, as lots of species are more active and easier to spot when the weather starts to warm up.

Here are two fun activities you can try when you go out for a walk this season. One is all about the creatures that live under the water, and one is all about the birds that live on or near it.

Pond dipping

Pond dipping is a brilliant way to explore creatures who live in fresh water.

You will need

- A pond dipping net
- A shallow plastic or metal tray
- A notepad and pencil (optional)
- A magnifying glass (optional)

Staying safe: always have an adult close by when you are pond dipping, and never wade into the water or lean over it. Make sure you keep your hands away from your face and wash them when you get home.

What to do

1. Ask your grown-up to help you find a place where you can safely stand near the edge of the water.

2. Start by looking carefully into the water. Can you see or hear any creatures moving around? This can give you clues as to where you should use your net.

3. Ask your grown-up to gently dip the tray into the water to capture a small amount of water.

4. Lower your net into the water, slowly and carefully. Move it through the water slowly in a figure-of-eight pattern a few times, then lift it out of the water.

5. Put the net in your tray and carefully turn it inside out, so that anything you have caught goes into the water in the tray. Check your net to make sure there are no creatures still in there.

6. Take a good look at what you have caught. Remember to only observe and not touch. If you want to make any notes or sketches, you could do it now.

7. When you have finished, ask your grown-up to pour the contents back into the water.

Did you spot any of the common pond dwellers on the next page?

☐ Pond skater

☐ Frog

☐ Damselfly

☐ Dragonfly

☐ Water beetle

☐ Newt

☐ Pond snail

☐ Water boatman

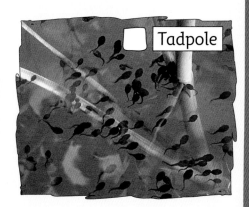

☐ Tadpole

Water bird spotting

Water birds swim or wade in water, and usually build their nests on the ground or in reeds.

Spring is nesting season for lots of water birds. If you go for a walk along a river or near a pond in spring, you might see water birds hard at work looking after their young.

Staying safe: it's very important to only watch wild birds and their nests, so never get too close or try to touch them. They may see you as a threat and act aggressively, especially if they have eggs or chicks to protect.

Look out for birds that are:
• **Building a nest.** These could be on the banks of the water, or among reeds and plants growing in the water. Birds are very clever at hiding their nests so you might need to look hard to find them.

• **Sitting on a nest.** This is because the female bird has laid her eggs in the nest, and the eggs need to be kept warm and safe in order to hatch.

• **Looking after baby chicks:** Babies need lots of care and attention, so the parent birds will be working hard. You might see the grown-ups finding food and giving it to the chicks, rounding them up when they swim too far away, or keeping them warm in the nest by tucking them under their feathers.

Can you spot any of these water birds while you're out and about?

Grey heron

Coot

Duck

Moorhen

Swan

Goose

33

10 | Magical, musical nature

If you have ever taken a stick and beat it on a log or tree stump you will know how much fun it is to create sound in the great outdoors.

Nature is full of its own music and a great place to make music too. Here are two fun ways to explore this.

Bee Breathing

Bee breathing is a musical breathing exercise. It's lovely to do outside in the freshest of fresh air.

How to do it

1. Take a long breath in through your nose as if you are smelling a flower.

2. Then let a slow breath out through your mouth, whilst making a continuous buzzing bee sound.

You can play around with this, making long noises and short noises, and you can even try it again with your hands covering your ears.

Thinking about your breath as you breathe in and out is called mindful breathing and it can actually be really good for you. Another benefit of bee breathing is that the vibrations are scientifically proven to help you feel calmer and less stressed.

Make a Grass Whistle

Making a grass whistle might take a little practice but once you can do it you will want to show everyone!

1. Pick a flat blade of grass that's as long as your thumb and is flat, wide and dry.

2. Straighten your thumbs and press them together at the knuckles, with your thumbnails facing you. Hold the grass lengthwise between your thumbs.

3. Make sure the grass is straight and taut.

4. Put your mouth close to your two thumbs, just below the knuckles, and blow. You might need to move your lips about and try different lengths of breath – keep trying!

5. Your breath makes the grass vibrate and create a loud sound.

11 | Nature postcards and bracelets

These nature postcards and bracelets are a fun way to make a walk more exciting. You can practise your nature-spotting skills and create your very own unique piece of nature art to take home.

You will need

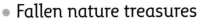

- A piece of card – a small rectangle for a postcard, or a long, thin strip for a bracelet

- Some double-sided sticky tape

- Scissors

- Fallen nature treasures

Making a nature postcard

1. Cut a strip of double-sided sticky tape that's as long as the longest edge of the card.

2. Peel off one side of the backing and stick the tape along the middle of the card. Leave the other side of the backing tape on for now.

3. Look for fallen nature treasure to decorate your postcard when out walking. When you find something, peel off a bit of the backing tape and stick your find to the postcard.

Making a nature bracelet

1. Trim your strip of card so that it wraps around your wrist with a little bit extra to overlap.

2. Cut a piece of double-sided sticky tape that's as long as the longest edge of the card.

3. Stick one side of the tape down the middle of the card. Leave the other side of the backing tape on for now.

4. When you're ready to wear your bracelet, peel off a little bit of backing tape at one end of the card. Wrap the card around your wrist, and stick the ends together to make a bracelet.

5. Now you're ready to head out for a walk and make your nature art. When you find fallen nature treasure, peel off a bit of backing tape and stick your find to the bracelet.

Always make sure you protect nature by only picking up things that have already fallen to the ground – don't pick things from trees or plants.

We can never have enough of nature.
Henry David Thoreau

12 | Elderflower foraging

Elderflowers can be found in hedgerows, in parks and by the sides of canals. They are usually ready for picking from early May to late June and are good to use in lots of recipes, where they give a lovely flowery, fruity taste.

As with all foraging it is important to only pick from public places, not private (like gardens), and always remember to leave lots behind!

How to forage elderflowers

• Take this book with you (or an image on a phone) so you can identify the flowers properly. You will also need a bag to put them in and a small pair of scissors.

• Pick your elderflowers on a dry day. If it's a little bit cloudy there will be fewer bugs.

• Only take a few flowers from each tree so you are leaving lots behind to turn into berries. These will feed the birds and insects later in the summer.

• Have a sniff. It's best to only pick the flowers that smell flowery. If they smell of cat wee (yuck) they are too ripe and are best left on the tree.

• Use the scissors to remove the flower heads, cutting just below the main stem belonging to the head of the flower. You want as little of the green stem in your recipes as possible.

• When you get the flowers home, give them a shake to remove insects (do this outside) then a little rinse with cold water.

Use them on the day you pick them. (Don't eat them raw, as this could make you ill.)

38

Elderflower shortbread

You will need

- 100 g cold butter/spread (you can use vegan substitutes instead)
- 50 g granulated sugar
- 150 g plain flour
- 3 tbsp of elderflowers, with stems removed
- Zest of 2 lemons

How to make it

1. Turn the oven on to 180 °C fan/gas mark 4.

2. Line a round cake tin with greaseproof paper.

3. Cut the butter/spread into chunks and put it in a mixing bowl with the sugar and flour.

4. Rub the ingredients together using your fingers until it forms breadcrumbs.

5. Add the lemon zest and elderflowers and mix everything together.

6. Use your hands to press the crumb mix into a soft dough.

7. Push the soft dough into the lined baking dish and prick it gently all over with a fork.

8. Bake for 25 minutes. It should be a very pale golden brown colour.

9. Once baked, remove the cake tin carefully from the oven and leave the shortbread to cool before cutting it into slices (with help from your grown-up). Take it out of the tin once it has completely cooled.

13 | Make a rangoli

Rangoli is a beautiful Indian folk art that involves creating a colourful pattern from flowers, sand, lentils, beans, spices, flour, colourful stones or leaves. It is usually made on the floor or on a table to welcome guests and to bless a home, but sometimes it is made out on the street. It is thought to bring good luck.

Some families make a rangoli every day, but lots of people save it for special festivals like Diwali, a five-day 'festival of lights' celebrated by Hindus all over the world.

Diwali takes place each year in either October or November, but since there aren't many flowers around in the UK at that time of year, we are going to make our rangoli in spring instead, when they are plentiful.

Rangoli designs are often symmetrical patterns that look like a large flower. They can be as simple or as complicated as you like.

How to make a flower rangoli

1. Search online for a design or create your own and practise drawing it on paper a few times till you're happy with it. You will be copying this later.

2. Head out for a nature walk and pick lots of the same types of leaves, some dandelions, daisies or other plentiful fallen flowers, or raid your own garden or the flower vase (with permission). Collect lots of small stones too.

3. After you get home, you might want to paint the stones you have collected in lots of lovely bright colours. Acrylic paint works well on stones.

4. Pull the petals off the flowers (unless they have small heads, in which case you can leave them intact).

5. Now chalk your design lightly onto the ground where you want to put your rangoli.

6. Once you are happy with the outline, simply fill your design with the flowers, stones and other items, aiming for harmony and symmetry.

After you've made your rangoli
Rangolis will often be swept away by the weather so take a photo to remember yours by. You could send it to friends and family who aren't nearby so they can enjoy your creation too.

Be aware!
Stones and flowers can be tripping hazards, so don't leave your rangoli on a path where someone could stumble on it. Be sure to remove the stones later.

41

Summer

Summer is here and there is no better time to be outside in nature.

School is out and so are the flowers and everywhere is in full bloom. These are days to head to the park, wander in the woods, visit a beach, and follow the trails.

Summer is an exciting time and full of adventure. It is time to camp and learn some awesome survival skills, skim stones, walk barefoot and celebrate the solstice. Maybe you want to pick fruit and get baking. Or perhaps you'd like to learn the names of all the trees (which is so much easier now that they have their leaves).

Perhaps you would like to try creating a community hopscotch or gathering all your friends for some brilliant park games? Insects abound in summer too, providing a wonderful opportunity to hunt for bugs.

You need never be bored with all the games and activities nature has to offer, so grab your friends, your family and a picnic and let's head off into the gorgeous summer months.

Heading down to the park with your family and friends may not sound the most original thing to do. But it can actually be the very best of times. All you need to make it special are some brilliant park games to play (and maybe a picnic too).

Here are some ideas for park games you may not have played before.

French Cricket

You will need

- A cricket bat or tennis racket

- A tennis ball or soft ball of similar size

- At least four people

How to play

1. Choose someone to bat. All other players are 'fielders' and make a circle around the batter, about 3 metres away.

2. The batter stands with their feet together, holding the bat in front of their legs (or 'stumps') to defend them.

3. The players in the circle take it in turns to bowl the ball at the 'stumps'.

4. If the batter hits the ball, they can move their feet and turn around to face another direction. If they miss, they have to twist to protect their 'stumps' without moving their feet.

5. If the ball hits either of the batter's legs below the knee, the batter is out and the person who bowled becomes the batter.

6. If the batter hits the ball and a fielder catches it before it bounces, the batter is out and the fielder that caught the ball becomes the batter.

7. The person who bats the most balls is the winner.

Detective

This is a fun game for a slightly larger group. You will need to be really quick if you want to fool the detective!

You will need

- At least eight players
- Space to move about

How to play

1. Stand in a circle about 2 metres apart and pick someone to be the 'detective'. Get the detective to move away so they cannot see or hear what is happening.

2. Now choose a leader. The leader chooses physical movements, like star jumps or hops, which the rest of the group will copy as soon as the leader starts.

3. Next, call the detective to come back and stand in the middle of the circle. They have to figure out who's the leader of the group in three guesses or less. If they get it right, the leader then becomes the detective, and the game continues. If they get it wrong, they stay as detective and start a new game.

Kick the Can

This game is a spin on hide and seek and much more exciting!

You will need

- An empty tin can
- Lots of safe places to hide nearby
- An area to the side marked off as 'prison'

How to play

1. Place an empty tin can on the ground and pick someone to be 'It'.

2. 'It' stands next to the tin can and counts to 50 while everyone else hides.

3. The player who is 'It' searches. When they spot someone, they call out their name and they both race to be the first to kick the can.

4. If 'It' kicks the can first, the hider becomes their prisoner and has to go to 'prison'.

5. If the hider kicks the can first, all players in prison are freed, and 'It' must count again.

> We are game-playing, fun-having creatures, we are the otters of the universe.
> **Richard Bach**

15 | Nature journalling

A nature journal is a book where you can write about your thoughts, feelings, activities and observations of nature. It is a fun way to watch the seasons unfold while on your walks and it has many benefits like helping you to develop observational skills, express how you feel, practise your writing and drawing skills, learn to be more mindful and explore nature.

- Small flowers or leaves
- Drawings of animals
- Photographs of trees
- One word that sums up your experience that day
- A painting of a rainbow

You will need

- A sturdy book with blank pages
- Pens, pencil, paint, glue
- Nature treasures

What to include

The thing about a journal is that it is entirely your own creation. Make it your own and do with it just as you wish. Here are some ideas to get you started:

SPEND TIME IN NATURE

July 10th

I love the lavender that grows in our front garden.
It smells of summer and looks so pretty.
The bees love it too.

Simply Brushes

July 21

today! Saw a rainbow

Red, Orange, Yellow, Green, Blue
Indigo & Violet

47

16 | Summer solstice activities

There are so many ways to celebrate the sun on your nature walk, and the summer solstice is the perfect time to do it.

The summer solstice is the longest day of the year, and it traditionally marks the start of summer. The timing of the solstice varies each year, but it generally occurs around 20, 21 or 22 June.

People all over the world have celebrated the summer solstice for thousands of years, honouring the sun and hoping for a good harvest. Here are two sun-worshipping activities you might like to try.

Sunshine meditation

Find somewhere outside where you can sit quietly with your legs crossed and hands resting gently in your lap.

Close your eyes and take three long, deep breaths. Imagine you are lying on gorgeous golden sand, with the sun shining down on you.

Give your toes a wiggle and your shoulders a shrug and let your body deeply relax. Imagine yourself getting up and taking a slow walk along the beach as the sun shines down, stopping to pick up shells, admire sandcastles and watch the blue waves lapping gently at the shore. After a while you turn and walk back. You say a thank you to the sun for your gorgeous walk and you curl up to sleep feeling warm and content.

Now raise your arms in the sky and have a good stretch, let out a long, slow breath and open your eyes.

You can take yourself somewhere sunny and peaceful any time you wish.

Make a sun print

You will need

- Leaves or flowers
- Sticky tape
- Coloured construction paper

How to make your print

1. Arrange your leaves or flowers on the paper and secure them with thin strips of sticky tape.

2. Use small stones to weigh the leaves or flowers down, or carefully cover them with the glass from a photo frame to keep them in place. Alternatively, you could stick the paper to a window that faces the sun. Pressing the leaves or flowers against the glass stops them from moving.

3. Leave the paper in the sun for a few hours, or a day or so if it's cloudy.

4. When you see that the colour of the exposed paper has faded, remove the leaves or flowers to reveal their silhouettes left on the paper.

> Wherever you go, no matter what the weather, always bring your own sunshine.
> Anthony J. D'Angelo

49

17 | Fruit picking

Fruit picking is a fun activity that can lead to some brilliant makes and bakes.

Do you have a fruit farm near you?

Ask around to find your nearest fruit farm or community garden, take a look online at their website, and then look carefully at their opening times. It might also be a good idea to have your grown-up call ahead, to find out the best time to visit and make sure they are well stocked.

It is way more fun to pick your own fruit than to shop for it at a supermarket!

Five things to know about picking fruit at a fruit farm:

1. You are not allowed to eat as you pick. You will need to wait until the fruit you have picked has been weighed before you can eat it (and remember, it will need to be washed first).

2. You have to pay for the fruit you pick, so be guided by your grown-up and don't pick more than you can eat or they can afford!

3. Check if you need to bring your own baskets or containers – the brilliant thing about picking your own fruit is that you aren't buying it wrapped in plastic that can harm the environment.

4. As well as reducing waste, picking your own is usually less expensive than buying from a shop, and you get to pick the very best of the crop. So do pick carefully and choose fruit that is ripe, but not too ripe.

5. Pick a cool day to go – it can be hard work in the heat!

To really make the most of your fruit-picking experience, why not have a go at using what you have picked in a recipe when you get back home?

Strawberry milkshake

We made our milkshake vegan, but if you aren't vegan you might want to use regular dairy milk and vanilla dairy ice-cream instead.

You will need

- 200 g strawberries
- 200 g (5 scoops) vegan vanilla ice-cream
- 200 ml oat milk

How to make it

1. Wash the ripe strawberries and pull out or cut off the stalks.

2. Place the strawberries, ice-cream and oat milk in a blender for 30 seconds. It should look smooth and creamy.

3. Pour into a cup and drink straight away while it's still cold.

Optional extras

- Ripe strawberries are usually really sweet, but if your milkshake doesn't taste sweet enough you could add a little maple syrup.

- If you wanted to make your milkshake super fancy you could add dairy-free whipped cream with sprinkles, sliced strawberries and chocolate shards.

18 Bug hunting

> **Around a flowering tree, one finds many insects.**
> Guinean proverb

Cool bug facts

- Insects have been on Earth for around 400 million years.

- Insects are invertebrates, which means they don't have bones like we do. Instead, they have a hard exoskeleton, or shell, to protect them.

- Nearly all insects hatch from eggs.

- Insects make up around 90 per cent of all animal life on Earth.

- For every person on Earth, there are about 1.4 billion insects!

While on your next walk, why not practise your nature detective skills with a bug hunt?

Tips for finding bugs

Bugs like to live in lots of different habitats. Some love shady, damp places, while others are happy in warmer, more exposed spots. If you explore a variety of habitats on your bug hunt you will find more types of minibeast.

Some great places to look are:

- In grass
- On leaves
- In soil
- Tree bark
- Under stones, twigs or logs
- Under plant pots
- On flowers

You will need

- A clear container with a lid
- A soft-bristled paintbrush
- Pencil and paper
- An old piece of fabric (optional)
- A magnifying glass (optional)
- Bug ID chart (optional)

On your bug hunt...

Your observation skills are very important for spotting bugs. You will need to look carefully, and be gentle when moving things to look for them.

You also need to be very careful when handling bugs. Use your soft-bristled paintbrush to gently sweep them into your clear container. Once they're in, put the lid on to stop them escaping while you study them. A magnifying glass is a brilliant way to see bugs in greater detail.

To use a piece of fabric to collect bugs, lay it out under a tree or bush and give the branches a gentle shake so that the bugs fall onto the fabric.

You might like to make a record of the types of bugs you find, and where you found them. If you're not sure what type of bug you've found you could use a bug ID chart or take a photo and look it up online when you get home.

When you've finished studying your bugs, carefully return them to the place you found them and replace any twigs or stones you've moved.

Variations

● It's fun to carry out a minibeast survey during your bug hunt. Count how many of each type of bug you find, and create a bar chart or graph from your results. For the bugs with high numbers, why do you think there are so many? What about the bugs with low numbers?

● Take a sketchbook on your bug hunt and draw your minibeasts. This is a good way to record any species that you want to look up later.

● Many bugs are at their most active in spring and summer, but you can have a go at bug hunting at any time of the year. If you do a bug hunt in the same place during a different season, what do you find?

19 | Hopscotch walk

Have you ever played hopscotch? It is such a simple game but lots of fun. You can play it with friends or on your own, and you simply need a stick of chalk, a stone and a paved area.

On your next walk, why not make a hopscotch course for you and anyone else passing by to play?

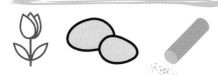

- Washable pavement chalk
- Pebbles
- Fallen nature (to decorate)
- To know how to draw a basic hopscotch course (see the picture).

On your walk

As you walk, collect up any bits of fallen nature for your hopscotch outline. These could include:

- Sticks
- Feathers
- Small flowers
- Leaves

Making your hopscotch course

Draw a hopscotch design on the ground with your chalk. Try to make your squares roughly the same size.

Hopscotch rules

1. Throw a pebble onto square 1.

2. If your pebble lands outside the square or on a line, your turn is over. If your pebble lands within square 1, jump over it to land with your feet on squares 2 and 3.

3. You then complete the course, hopping with one foot where there are single squares, and jumping with both feet onto the squares that are side by side.

4. Hop into square 10, turn around and complete the course back to the start, stopping to pick up the pebble on your way.

5. If you fall or miss a square at any point, play passes to the next person.

6. If you complete the course with no mistakes, it is the next person's turn. When it comes round to you again, you throw your pebble to square 2 and the next time to square 3 and so on.

Variations

If you are a little short of time or want to do something younger kids will enjoy, you could simply chalk a circle, decorate the outline with your nature finds then write inside 'Jump in and make a wish'.

It is a happy talent to know how to play.
Ralph Waldo Emerson

20 | Scavenger hunts

There's so much going on in nature at this time of year. Plants and trees are full of leaves and flowers, lots of tiny creatures are out and about, and there are lovely birds, butterflies and bees to enjoy.

Have a go at being a nature detective with these fun summer scavenger hunts. As well as a general nature hunt, there's one full of minibeasts to spot, and a beach-themed scavenger hunt which is perfect if you're visiting the seaside. Take your pick or have a go at all three!

You don't have to spot everything in one session – you can keep coming back to your list to tick things off whenever you find them.

Some things on the list are pretty small, so you might need to look carefully and think like a detective to find them!

The beauty of the natural world lies in the details.
Natalie Angier

Nature scavenger hunt

☐ Blue sky

☐ Clover leaf

☐ Daisy

☐ Duck

☐ Dandelion clock

☐ Green leaves

☐ Sunflower

☐ Squirrel (grey or red)

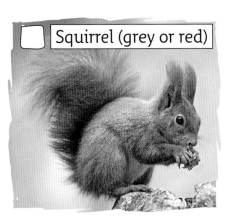

☐ A singing bird

Minibeasts scavenger hunt

☐ Ant

 ☐ Butterfly

☐ Bee

 ☐ Dragonfly

☐ Ladybird

☐ Caterpillar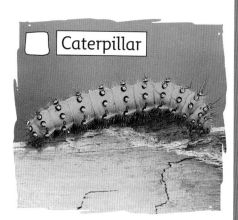

☐ Moth

 ☐ Snail

☐ Spider

Seaside scavenger hunt

☐ Crab

☐ Driftwood

☐ Feather

☐ Jellyfish
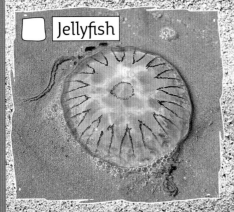

☐ Gull

☐ Seaweed

☐ Shell

☐ Starfish

☐ Waves

21 | Camping games and activities

Camping is a brilliant way to get in touch with nature because you're outside for most of the day. And that means you can have fun with lots of outdoor games and activities.

Here are some fun ideas that are perfect for a camping trip. If you're not going camping this summer, you can still have a go at them while on a walk in the park or countryside.

Camping Games

Human Knot

1. Everyone stands in a circle.

2. Each person has to reach out and join hands with two different people. Each left hand needs to hold another left hand, and each right hand needs to hold another right hand.

3. When everyone is holding two other hands, the group has to try and unravel itself without anyone letting go of the hands they are holding. You will need to work together.

4. When the human knot is untangled, everyone will be standing in a circle.

Commando

1. Choose one person to be the 'counter'. Everyone else is a 'runner'.

2. Decide on a start/finish zone, then choose six checkpoints in a circle around it. Checkpoints can be objects you place on the ground, or things like trees and bushes.

3. The counter calls out a number between 5 and 10, then says 'fast', 'medium' or 'slow' and closes their eyes.

> "Now I see the secret of making the best persons, it is to grow in the open air and to eat and sleep with the earth.
> Walt Whitman

4. The counter keeps their eyes shut while counting down from the number they called out to zero. The 'fast', 'medium' or 'slow' dictates the speed at which they do this.

5. Starting from the start/finish point, the runners have to tag all the checkpoints and get back to the start/finish without the counter seeing them.

6. When the counter reaches zero, they open their eyes and call out the names of runners that they can see. If a runner is spotted, they are out.

7. The counter then calls out another number and begins counting down again until there is only one runner left.

What's the Time, Mr Wolf?

1. Choose someone to be the wolf.

2. The wolf stands at one end of an open space and turns their back to everyone. All other players stand at the other end of the space.

3. The players call out, 'What's the time, Mr Wolf?'. The wolf then turns around and calls out a time, for example, 'Two o'clock'. The players take that number of steps towards the wolf.

4. This is repeated until the wolf decides to call out, 'It's dinner time!'. When the wolf does this, the players can run away back to their starting point while the wolf tries to catch one of them.

5. If a player is caught they become the wolf and the game restarts.

63

Campfire Fun

Hot Potato

1. Everyone sits in a circle.

2. One person (this can be a grown-up) sits out of the game and is in charge of playing music in the background.

3. While the music is playing, the players must pass the 'hot potato' (a ball or small object) around the circle.

4. When the music stops, the player holding the hot potato is out – so don't hang onto it for long!

5. If you drop the hot potato you are also out.

6. The last person left is the winner.

Storytelling

To create a brilliant group story, you need these five things:

1. PLACE. Where is the story set?

2. TIME. What season, what time of day is it?

3. CHARACTER. Think about who your main character is. What do they look like? What are their skills and interests?

4. QUEST. Give your main character a quest to make your story exciting. For example, they could be searching for something, rescuing someone, solving a mystery or fighting for a cause.

5. IDEAS. How is your main character going to tackle their quest? Think about obstacles they might come across.

Creating your group story

Starting with 'place', come up with ideas for each of the five things on the list. It's fun to discuss and add to each other's suggestions as you go along.

If there are lots of you, it might help to appoint a storyteller. Their job is to put the story together and keep track of it. They can make sure everyone gets a turn, and ask people to add details or expand on ideas. The storyteller can also keep telling the story so far, to help everyone remember where you've got to.

When your story is finished, all you need to do is give it a title and it's ready to send out into the world!

S'mores recipe

S'mores are a traditional campfire treat and the perfect accompaniment to a storytelling session.

You will need

- Plain biscuits
- A bar of milk chocolate
- Marshmallows
- Aluminium foil

Vegan chocolate and gelatine-free marshmallows also work well.

How to make S'mores

1. Tear a square of aluminium foil that's big enough to wrap two biscuits in.

2. Put one biscuit on the foil, add the chocolate and top with marshmallows. Put another biscuit on top.

3. Use the foil to wrap around your biscuit.

4. Ask a grown-up to put the foil parcel on the campfire or barbecue for about 2 minutes on each side.

5. Once the foil parcel has been removed from the fire, leave it to cool for a few minutes. The chocolate and marshmallows should be melted and gooey – delicious!

22 | Games of stones

Stones are one of the best things ever to play games with. They are easy to find, free and everywhere!

Stone Toss

This is a game for two or more players and is a great way to test your aiming skills. You will need to create a small hole in the ground – loose soil or sand works best (don't dig up the garden though!). Make the hole about the width of a cereal bowl.

You will need

- Six small stones for each player

How to play

1. Decide on where the throwing spot will be. The further away from the hole it is, the harder the game.

2. The players take turns to stand on the throwing spot and toss one of their stones into the hole in the ground.

3. The person who gets the most stones in the hole is the winner.

Hotter Colder

This is a hiding game that has been played for decades with all sorts of objects.

You will need

- An unusual looking stone (either very big or an odd shape or colour)

- At least two players (one the hider, one the hunter)

How to play

1. The hider shows the hunter the stone they are going to hide, then the hunter goes away whilst the hider places it out of sight.

2. The hunter then returns and starts to look around for the stone.

3. When the hunter gets close, the hider shouts out words like 'hot', 'hotter' or 'really hot!', depending on how close to the stone they are. When the hunter moves away from the hiding place or looks in the wrong place, the hider shouts 'cold', 'colder' or 'freezing!', depending on how far away they are.

4. Once the stone has been found, the hider becomes the hunter, and the hunter becomes the hider.

Tower Race

Tower games are great fun and test your patience and balancing skills.

You will need

- Stones of various shapes and sizes

How to play

For one player:

Gather up a pile of stones of various sizes. Time yourself as you build a tower by placing one on top of the other. Have another go and try to beat your time.

For two players:

Gather up a pile of ten stones, each of different sizes. Race to see who can build their tower first. It has to stand for at least 10 seconds in order for you to win!

"I alone cannot change the world, but I can cast a stone across the waters to create many ripples."
Mother Teresa

23 Tree identification

There are over 60,000 different tree species on our planet – have you ever thought about how many types of tree grow where you live?

This fun tree identification activity will help you learn more about nature on your doorstep.

One easy way to identify trees is by looking at their leaves. Each type of tree has its own particular shape, size and colour of leaves.

Amazing leaf facts
• Leaves are responsible for the process of photosynthesis. This is how plants make their own food from sunlight, water and carbon dioxide.

As part of photosynthesis, trees remove carbon dioxide from the air and produce oxygen, so they play a very important role in keeping our air breathable. Trees are often referred to as 'the lungs of the planet'.

• Some trees lose their leaves in winter; these are called deciduous trees. Evergreen trees keep their leaves all year.

• Many types of tree leaves change colour in autumn. It is the chlorophyll in their leaves that makes them green, and when the levels of chlorophyll drop in autumn, other colours such as orange, brown and red start to become visible.

• There are over 400 times more trees on Earth than there are people!

Identifying trees
Here are leaves from some common trees. Can you spot them all?

Variations
In autumn, lots of trees produce seeds or seed pods. This makes it a great time to have a go at a different way of identifying trees. You could create your own tree identification chart by looking online for images of seeds, then heading out to see what you can find.

"Time spent amongst trees is never wasted time."
Katrina Mayer

Ash

Beech

Alder

Elder

Field maple

Cherry

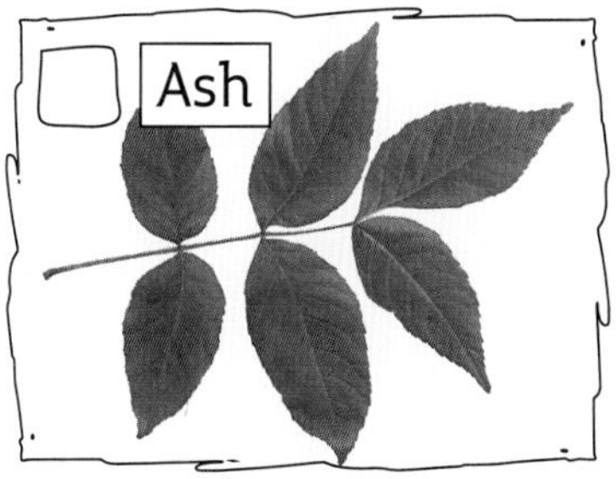

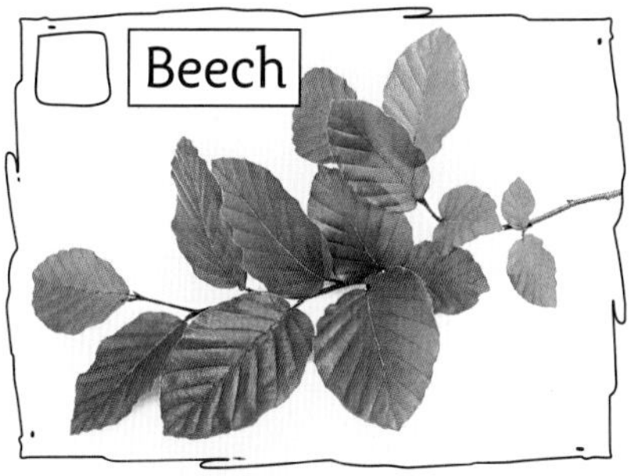

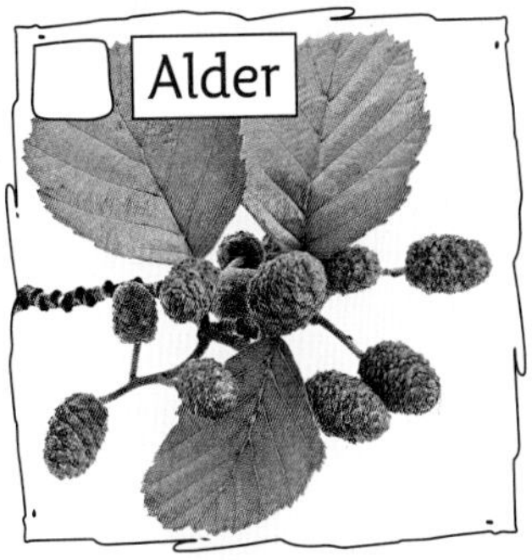

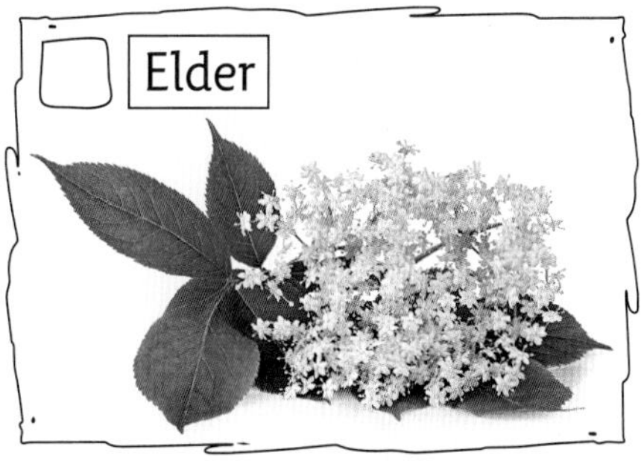

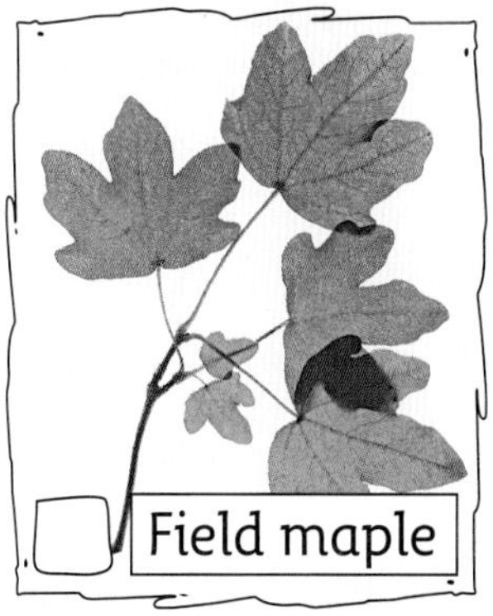

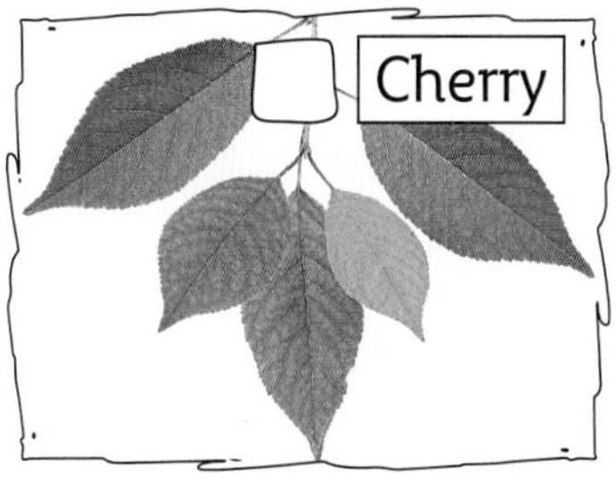

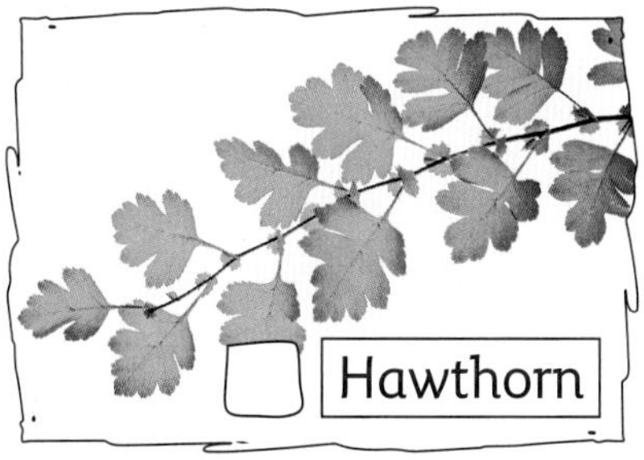

Hawthorn

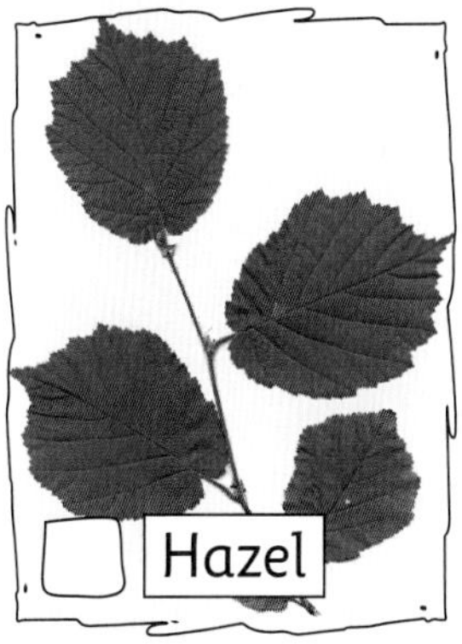

Hazel

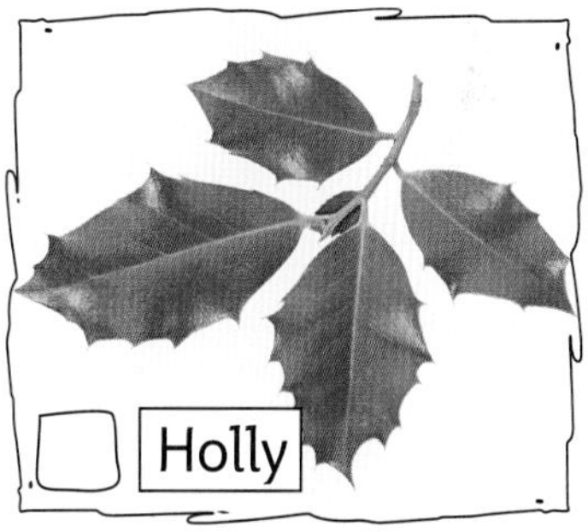

Holly

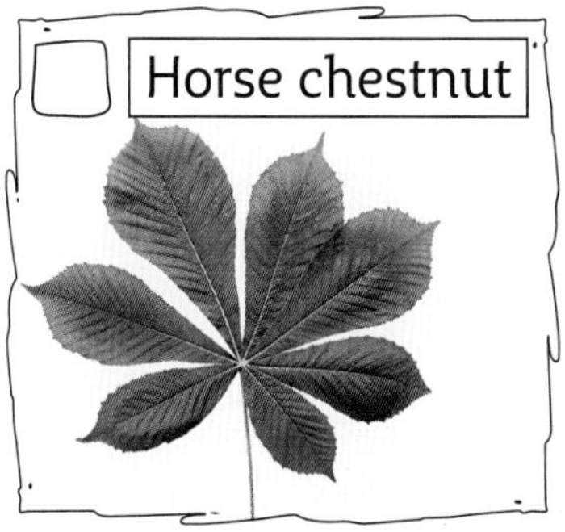

Horse chestnut

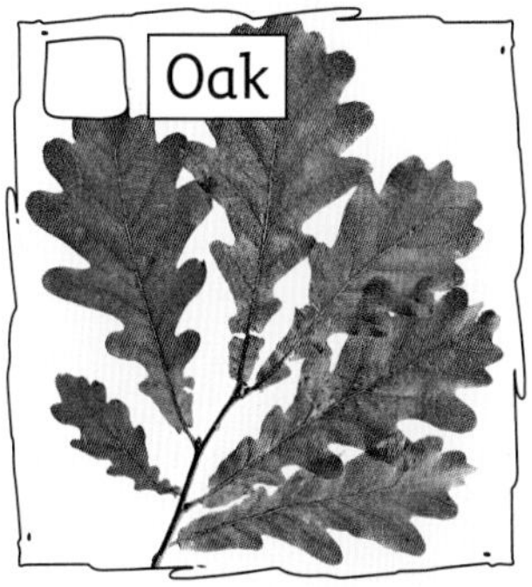

Oak

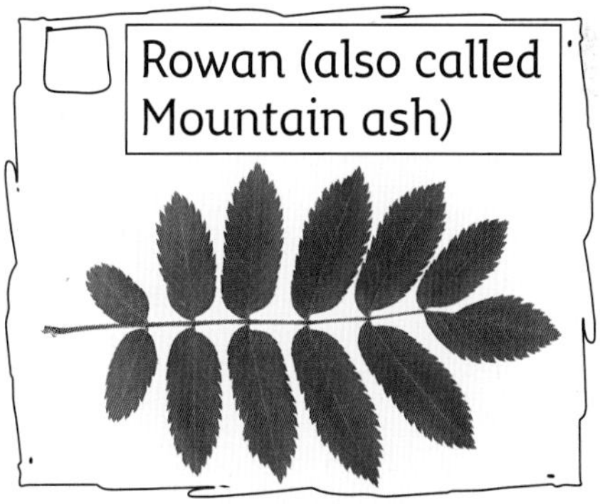

Rowan (also called Mountain ash)

Scots pine

Silver birch

Sycamore

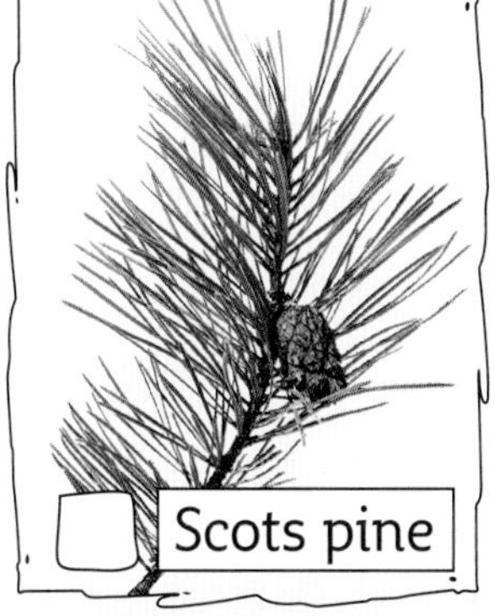

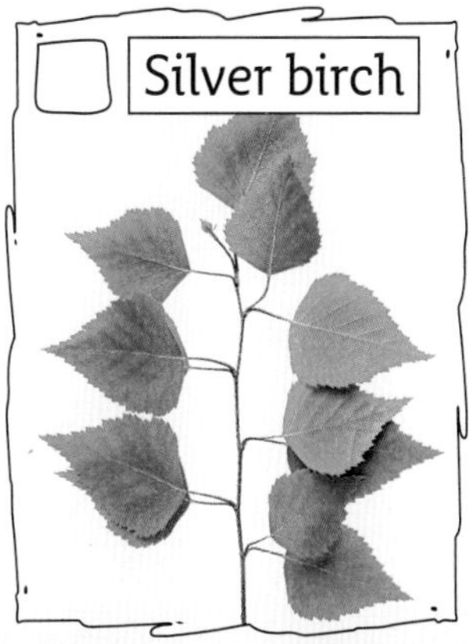

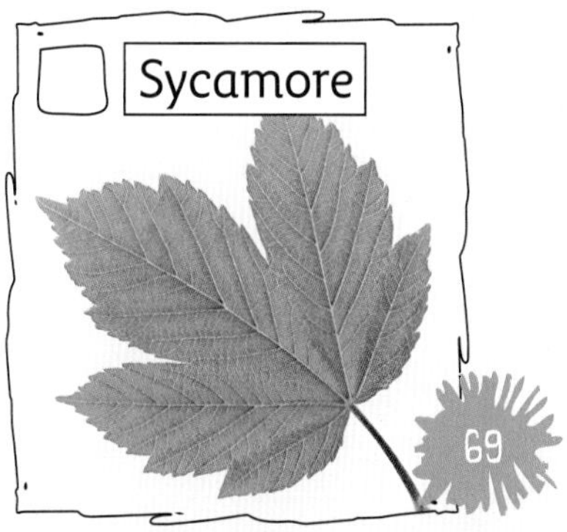

24 Litter picking

Litter is really bad for nature. It is dangerous to wildlife, it can prevent plants from growing well, and it can pollute soil, water and air.

Picking up litter and disposing of it correctly is an easy way to look after nature, and you'll be helping your local community too.

Litter facts

• Food and drink packaging makes up a large proportion of litter.

• A lot of litter that is thrown away on land ends up in our oceans. It's estimated that by 2050 there could be more plastic in the world's oceans than fish.

• Dealing with litter costs a huge amount of money – over £500 million a year in Britain alone. Think about how many ways we could help people and nature with this money if we didn't have to spend it on cleaning up!

What you can do

You could organise your own litter pick, join in with a local volunteer group, or perhaps even get your school involved.

Lots of local councils provide equipment for litter picking, and may even collect the bags of litter after your event. So before you start litter picking, it's worth contacting your local council to find out if they can help.

You will need

- Protective gloves

- A bag or bucket for collecting litter

- A litter picker (optional)

Litter picking tips

- You should always have an adult with you while litter picking.

- Only litter pick on public land, or private land if you have permission from the land owner.

- You need to wear suitable clothing and shoes for your litter pick. It's also a good idea to check the weather forecast – you might need waterproofs or sun cream.

- Always wear protective gloves when litter picking, and keep your hands away from your face.

- If possible, separate the litter you collect into different bags: one for recyclable items and one for general waste.

- Don't pick up sharp objects, such as broken glass, or things that might be hazardous such as chemical containers, electrical items and clinical waste. If you're not sure, check with your grown-up. You can report dangerous items to your local council.

- When you've finished litter picking, dispose of your bags of litter in your household waste or recycling bins.

- Wash your hands thoroughly after litter picking.

Variations

Once you've got the hang of litter picking, you could get in the habit of doing it whenever you go for a walk. Carry protective gloves and a rubbish bag with you, so you're ready to take action when you spot some litter.

Another important place to tackle litter is at the beach. Over 8 million tonnes of litter enters our oceans every year, and lots of it washes up on the shoreline. Could you help to keep our oceans healthy by organising a beach clean-up next time you visit the seaside?

Practising basic outdoor survival skills while on your walk is a very good idea. Knowing what to do in unexpected situations gives us a much better chance of staying safe.

Camouflage

Camouflage involves blending into your surroundings so that you can't be easily spotted – or caught! Lots of animals use it to hide from predators or creep up on prey.

If you're playing an outdoor game with friends that involves hiding or tracking, here are some fun ways to camouflage yourself.

1. Wear green or brown clothes. If you mimic the colours of nature you will be harder to spot.

2. Make a pile of grass, fallen leaves, twigs or moss, and hide in it. Long grass also makes a brilliant hiding place.

3. Don't move. Our eyes are very good at noticing movement, so staying still or moving very slowly reduces your chances of being seen.

4. Get muddy! You can use wet mud to camouflage your face and hands. Make sure you check this is okay with a grown-up first.

Make a shelter

In the wild, a shelter protects you from the weather and helps to keep you safe from predators. You can practise making a shelter in the garden, park or woods.

You will need

- Strong, straight sticks or fallen branches
- A tree
- Leaves, mud and moss

How to make a shelter

1. Find two trees that are close together and place long sticks between them to make a roof.

2. Make sure the ground is flat and clear of stones.

3. Build up the sides of your shelter with more sticks or branches. Aim for a tent shape.

4. If you want to make your shelter stronger and waterproof, you can weave bendy sticks horizontally in and out of the upright sticks, then cover the whole den with leaves, twigs and moss.

5. Use fallen leaves to make a soft floor inside your shelter, or pop a blanket or sleeping bag in there.

6. Before going inside, make sure your shelter is secure by giving it a wiggle – you don't want it to collapse on you.

Signalling

Signalling is really useful when other people are too far away to hear you.

Easy ways to send a signal

1. Use a small mirror to reflect a beam of daylight. You can interrupt this beam with your hand to make a flashing effect.

2. Use a whistle. Agree with your friends what different whistle blasts mean before you split up. For example, three short blasts might mean 'I'm lost, please come and find me!'

3. Make a simple flag. Tie a piece of ribbon or a scrap of fabric to a stick and wave it to attract attention.

For more activities that involve survival skills, have a look at foraging (page 38), tracking (page 108), map reading (page 130) and using a compass (page 116).

26 | Mindfulness walk

What is mindful walking?

Mindfulness is when you focus on what is happening in the here and now, paying complete attention to your thoughts and feelings, your senses and the environment around you. It is really good to be mindful because it stops your brain from worrying about things that have happened before or things that are happening later, and this makes you feel much calmer and more peaceful.

A barefoot walk

Walking barefoot is a wonderful way to connect with nature and fully experience it. From sand to pebbles, grass to mud, your senses will be delighted and fully alert as you wander over so many different textures.

You can create your own temporary barefoot walk on any path or trail. Here's how:

1. Clear the area you plan to walk on to make sure there are no nasties waiting to trip you up or hurt your feet (like bottle tops or sharp stones). You could use branches to sweep the area.

2. Next, use sticks to mark out a path on the ground and divide it into sections.

3. Now search for different materials for each section, such as grasses, dandelions, fallen leaves, smooth stones, little sticks, flowers, squelchy wet soil, bark, a bowl of water, or even lavender. (Note that you shouldn't pick flowers if you are in the countryside or a park.)

4. Be sure to clear it all away when you are done.

Things to consider

You might want to encourage your family and friends to experience this walk too. Or maybe you want to have a go at doing it backwards or blindfolded!

How does it feel to walk on such different surfaces? Which one was your favourite?

As well as helping you feel more connected to nature, there are lots of other benefits to going barefoot. It improves your balance, body awareness and foot strength as your feet work hard balancing as you walk across unusual surfaces.

Wherever you are,
be there totally.
Eckhart Tolle

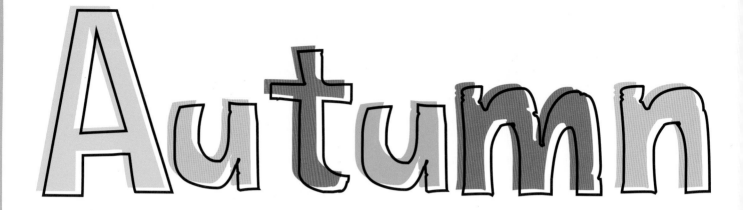

Autumn

Autumn in nature is a magical time of change. We can see the most wonderful things every time we step outside.

Colourful leaves float down from the trees, there are lots of lovely flowers to enjoy, and animals and insects scurry around preparing for winter. The autumn sunshine is still warm, and we can collect conkers and pine cones for games and crafts, or gather fruits and vegetables for a harvest celebration.

You can head out for a walk and try some wildlife tracking, measuring, and leaf challenges, or even go for a night walk to see nature in a whole different light.

We've got plenty of games and activities to keep you busy too. You could fly a kite on a windy day, search out shapes in nature, make a sound map or give your brain a workout with some nature riddles. There's lots of Halloween-themed nature fun in store too.

Grab your coat and pull on your wellies, it's time to enjoy the autumn show!

27 | Autumn riddle scavenger hunt

Autumn is a fantastic season to hunt for nature treasure. Plants, trees, animals and insects are adapting to the cooling temperatures and shortening days, and that means there are lots of interesting things to collect.

This autumn scavenger hunt can be done anywhere outdoors, and there's a bit of a twist to it: for every item on the list, you have to solve a riddle to work out what it is before you can find it.

When you've found each item, tick it off – you don't have to do them all in one go. If it takes the whole of autumn, that's absolutely fine.

The answers are at the bottom of the page if you get stuck!

1. I might be big, or rather small;
in autumn you will see me fall.

2. I am a seed; you'll know my name.
I'm often used to play a game.

3. You can ruffle me, write with me
and use me to tickle someone!

4. I'm red, orange, purple or black;
wildlife thinks I'm a tasty snack.

5. My first is in *beam*, but not in *tame*.
My second is in *pine*, but not in *open*.
My third is in *over*, but not in *love*.
My fourth is in *send*, but not in *nose*.

6. I'm stronger than steel but light as
a feather; if flies pay a visit, they're
stuck forever.

7. You can turn me into a sword, a
wand, a wind chime, a boat or a den –
or throw me for a dog to fetch!

"Out yonder there was this huge
world, which exists independently
of us human beings and which
stands before us like a great,
eternal riddle."
Albert Einstein

8. I can be red or grey, and like to climb;
I gather nuts in autumn time.

9. Bees love me; I'm often a gift. Some
people sneeze after I've been sniffed.

10. I carry my home wherever I go;
I like to glide but I'm pretty slow.

11. I have bark but I'm not a dog;
if you cut me down, I become a log.

12. You can jump in me as you pass
by; if you look when I'm still, you
might see the sky.

ANSWERS: 1. Leaf, 2. Conker, 3. Feather, 4. Berry,
5. Bird, 6. Spider's web, 7. Stick, 8. Squirrel,
9. Flower, 10. Snail, 11. Tree, 12. Puddle

79

28 | All about apples

Apples are one of the best things about autumn and, besides eating them raw, there are lots of fun things you can do with them!

Baked apples

Baked apples are delicious and easy to make, too.

You will need

- 4 ripe eating apples
- 2 handfuls of raisins
- 2 tbsp light brown sugar
- 1½ tsp cinnamon
- 25 g butter or plant-based spread
- 2 tsp demerara sugar

How to make them

1. Turn the oven on to 180 °C fan gas mark 6.

2. Carefully core the apples with an apple corer – you might need your grown-up to help with this.

3. Mix your raisins, brown sugar and cinnamon together in a small bowl.

4. Stand the apples side by side in a deep baking dish.

5. Add the raisin mix to each apple, pushing it down into the hole where the core was.

6. Add butter/spread to the top of each apple and sprinkle with demerara sugar.

7. Place in the oven for 20 minutes.

8. To check if the apples are ready, ask a grown-up to poke one with a knife or skewer – the apple should feel soft.

9. The apples will be red hot so ask your grown-up to remove them from the oven and let them cool down before serving.

> Even if I knew that tomorrow the world would go to pieces, I would still plant my apple tree.
> Martin Luther

Apple bird feeders

Birds love fruit, bird seed and nuts so you just know these bird feeders will go down a treat.

You will need

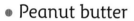

- String or twine
- Apples
- Bird seed
- Peanut butter

How to make them

1. Slice the apples (or ask your grown-up to) into about five slices from the top down, across the core.

2. Using a cutlery knife, carefully cut a hole out of the middle of each slice, making sure to get rid of any seeds (apple seeds aren't good for birds).

3. Now thread a piece of string through each hole and tie a knot to make a hanging loop. Use enough string so it can be hung on a branch.

4. Smear each slice with peanut butter and sprinkle on some bird seed. Press the seed gently into the peanut butter to make it stick.

5. Now simply hang the apple slices from your nearest tree and wait for the birds to spot them!

29 | Shape seeking

It is easy to walk past a tree or a berry, a stone or a stick and just take it for granted, not really seeing it at all. But look closely and you will see that nature is amazing and is created from the most beautiful shapes. Peer in and you will find that pine cones are made up of many little squares, spider's webs contain perfect rectangles, and blackberries are piled-up circles of fruit.

You will also see shapes formed by nature: a perfect hole made by the wind piercing a leaf, a cross made by interwoven branches, a triangle created by fallen sticks.

Looking for shapes in nature encourages you to look closer and see how wonderful it truly is. Are you ready to go shape seeking?

> If you truly love nature, you will find beauty everywhere.
> Vincent Van Gogh

How to shape seek

Choose a shape
You could have a theme for your shape seeking, such as circles, and try to spot as many as you can whilst out on your nature walk. You could have a competition with your friends or family to see who finds the most, or search together until you have found ten. Maybe you could snap a photo or do a quick sketch of what you see?

Shape-seeking bingo
Another way to shape seek is to try and spot all the shapes on our shape-seeking bingo board below. You are going to have to look hard to find some of them.

Triangle	Square	Circle
Rectangle	Star	Oval
Heart	Cross	Semicircle

Take a look at the photos to see our attempt at shape-seeking bingo! Have fun shape seeking!

Circle

Cross

Oval

Rectangle

Semicircle

Square

Triangle

Heart

Star

83

30 | Collect and dissect

Dissection is the scientific word for taking something apart so that you can examine it. It's a good way to study an object and learn how it works.

This experiment is all about collecting fallen nature treasures, then dissecting them to find out more about them. Autumn is a brilliant time of year to do this because there will be lots of interesting things to collect and study.

Collecting your specimens

You can collect your natural items anywhere – in the woods, on the way to school, in the park, in a garden or on any walk where you come across nature.

You could keep an eye out for interesting things when you're out and about, or make a special trip for a collecting session. Take a bag with you to store your treasures until you get home.

Flowers, leaves and acorns are all perfect for this activity.

You should only collect things that have already fallen to the ground – don't pick anything from plants or trees. Make sure you stay safe too; don't wander off from your grown-up, don't try to pick things up from roads and always wash your hands when you get home.

You will need

- Fallen nature treasures
- A piece of card or paper, or a paper plate
- Scissors
- Tweezers
- A magnifying glass (optional)

Dissecting and studying flowers

1. Place your flower on your paper or card.

2. Use your fingers, scissors or tweezers to gently separate the different parts of the flower.

3. See if you can identify these parts – you might like to label them:
- Petal – designed to attract insects (can you explain how?).
- Pollen – part of how the plant makes new flowers.
- Stem – carries nutrients and water from the soil to the flower.
- Leaf – uses sunlight to make oxygen and glucose (sugar) to feed the plant (this process is called *photosynthesis*).

4. You could also look up a diagram of flower parts and see if there is anything else you can identify.

Dissecting and studying leaves

1. Place your leaf on your paper or card.

2. See if you can identify these parts (sometimes it is easier to identify them if you look at the underside of the leaf):

- Stalk – attaches the leaf to the plant or tree.
- Tip – the opposite end from the stalk.
- Midrib – this is a tube running from the stalk down the centre of the leaf. It carries nutrients and water from the stalk to the veins.
- Veins – these are small lines that branch off from the midrib. They deliver the water and nutrients from the midrib to the leaf.
- Lamina – this is the main surface area of the leaf, containing the midrib and veins. It carries out photosynthesis.

3. Use your fingers, scissors or tweezers to gently dissect the leaf. You could cut across the stalk and study the cross-section, or cut away the lamina to create a leaf skeleton.

Dissecting and studying acorns

1. If the acorn still has a cap attached, remove it.

2. Ask a grown-up to use a knife to cut the acorn in half.

3. Place the cap and nut on your paper or card.

4. See if you can identify these parts:
- Stalk – attaches the acorn to the tree.
- Cupule – the little cap at the base of the acorn.

- Nut – made up of the outer shell (called the fruit wall), the seed coat (a layer inside the shell that protects the seed) and the embryo (the actual seed).
- Style – the little pointy bit on the end of the acorn.

5. Some things to think about:
- The shell will be tough and hard – why do you think this is?
- The inside of the nut will be soft – can you see any particular features? You might like to look up an acorn diagram to help you identify them.
- Why do you think the acorn has a cap?

31 | Make a nature sound map

Nature is absolutely jam-packed with sounds if you start to listen in.

Concentrating on what you can hear is a great way to develop your observational skills, and it can also help you to relax and feel less stressed. Paying attention to the sounds around you is often used as part of mindfulness practice for this very reason.

Next time you're out and about in nature, have a go at this sound map activity. If you take some time to really focus on what you can hear, you might be surprised by just how many things you hadn't noticed before – and how lovely it makes you feel.

You will need

- Some paper
- A pen or pencil
- Your ears!

How to make it

1. Start by finding a nice quiet place in nature. This could be in the park, in a garden, at the beach, or simply on the street where you live.

2. Draw yourself, or write an X, in the middle of your piece of paper. This is your sound map, and your job is to add sounds to the map to build up a picture of everything you can hear.

3. Sit down, relax, and start to focus on the sounds around you. It can help to close your eyes. The weather, animals, insects, water, and of course humans, all make noise outdoors. Even plants can be noisy when the wind blows or the rain falls on them.

4. When you hear a sound, draw it on the paper in the place you think it came from in relation to where you are. Remember that we're trying to concentrate on listening here, so a

simple drawing is all that's needed. For example, you could draw musical notes for birdsong, or drops of water for rain. It's fine to include man-made noises too if you want to.

5. When you've finished, think about how sitting quietly and listening has made you feel.

Questions to explore

- Are you surprised by anything on your map?

- How many of the sounds do you think you would have noticed usually?

- Did you hear anything that you couldn't actually see?

- Can a friend or a grown-up guess what the sounds are on your map?

Variations

Try making a sound map in the same place each season, or in the same place at different times of the day. What do you notice that's different? Is anything the same?

Could you make a sound map when it's dark? You will probably find that not being able to see as well makes your sense of hearing stronger. You could even combine this with the night walk activity on page 94.

> The Earth has its music for those who will listen.
> Reginald Holmes

All of these fun ideas are perfect for making a woodland walk more exciting.

1. Listen out for birdsong (and perhaps record it on a phone and work out which birds you have heard when you get home).

2. Use a magnifying glass to get up close to a fallen log – what can you spot?

3. Collect fallen nature treasures to make a collage.

4. Make mud pies.

5. Look for animal tracks.

6. Use a stick to draw a circle on bare ground, then take it in turns to try and throw a stone or pine cone into the circle.

7. Watch the clouds and the sky through the trees.

8. Find the perfect stick.

9. Make a tower out of stones.

10. Do some bird spotting and try to identify the species you see.

11. Have a go at bark rubbing.

12. See who can find the biggest leaf.

13. Carry out a nature survey.

14. Make a journey stick of your walk by attaching nature treasures to a twig with a piece of string.

15. Identify trees from their leaves.

16. Play 'I Spy'.

> "I took a walk in the woods and came out taller than the trees."
> Henry David Thoreau

17. Try forest bathing.

18. Make a nature mandala on the ground from fallen leaves, petals, twigs or stones.

19. Go for a woodland walk at night with a torch – what can you see and hear?

20. Do some litter picking.

21. Search for feathers to make a mobile or a pen.

22. Follow your route on a map or on a phone app.

23. Use a stick to tap out a rhythm on a tree trunk or rock.

24. Take a sketchbook and draw what inspires you.

25. Jump in a muddy puddle.

26. Have a woodland picnic.

27. Play hide and seek.

28. Use sticks and leaves to make a woodland trail for others to follow.

29. Concentrate on your senses: what can you hear, see, touch, smell?

30. Balance on a fallen log.

31. Look for signs of animal homes.

32. Make a fairy house.

33. Play 'follow the leader'.

34. Make a den.

35. Hug a tree!

36. Collect fallen flowers and press them when you get home.

37. Make a stick maze, then find your way out.

38. Count the rings on a tree stump to work out how old the tree is (each ring = 1 year).

39. Have a creepy crawly scavenger hunt.

40. Use a stick to play noughts and crosses in the dirt.

41. Hunt for pine cones.

42. Scatter some bird seed for wild birds to enjoy.

43. Have a go at mindful walking.

44. Fill an empty egg box with fallen nature bits and bobs.

45. Write a nature journal.

46. Take a book, sit down and enjoy some quiet reading time.

47. Keep count of how many different types of living thing you see.

48. Take a camera and photograph nature.

49. Climb a tree.

50. Make a stick man.

33 | Autumn leaves walk

Why not take a walk today and gather up some gorgeous autumn leaves?

Autumn leaves provide endless opportunities for fun. You can pile them into a huge heap and run and jump into them. You can take some home and make brilliant crafts from them. You can dissect them, paint them or you can even try and identify what kind of tree they have fallen from. So many uses!

Here are our favourite leaf projects.

Make a leaf wand

At the start of your walk, find a long, slim but strong stick. As you walk, thread on the best leaves that you find. You might want to go for all large leaves or all orange leaves or maybe a mix. Encourage every member of your group to do the same; you might be surprised by how different your wands look.

When you get home, put your leaf wand into a vase for a beautiful display (it's cheaper than a bunch of flowers and just as pretty!).

If you have a neighbour or older relative who doesn't get out much, consider gifting them a leaf wand to bring a bit of autumn's treasure into their home.

Anyone who thinks fallen leaves are dead has never watched them dancing on a windy day.
Shira Tamir

Make a leaf rainbow

This community art project is great fun to make and is sure to make passers-by smile. You will need to do it on a day that isn't windy, otherwise it will just blow away!

Take five bags with you on your walk and collect different-coloured leaves as you go, popping them into the bags according to their colour. Remember to only take fallen leaves.

Look out for leaves in these colours:

- Brown
- Green
- Red
- Yellow
- Orange

When you feel you have enough leaves, look for a big enough clearing to make your rainbow. It should be in a place where as many people as possible will see it, but not on a pathway as the leaves would make it slippy if it rained.

Begin the outer arc of your rainbow with red leaves if possible, then orange, yellow, green and lastly brown.

If you can't find enough different-coloured leaves, see what other fallen nature finds you could use instead.

34 | Night walking

Walking at night is so different to walking during the day. Darkness changes the world completely. You might find it a little scary at first but you soon get used to it and then it becomes exciting!

You could walk around your local area and see and hear how very different it is at night. Can you spot any animals? We live near a canal and sometimes see a fox dart across a road.

You could explore even further, walk around a woodland path or across fields. Chances are, if you are near some trees, you might hear an owl hoot, or if you go out and about in the late summer months you might see bats swooping around. Do take a grown up with you for safety when you adventure out into the dark.

Things to see and do at night

Stargazing

Away from the light pollution caused by streetlamps and houses, stars can shine much more clearly. So a night walk in a wood, on a beach, on a grassy hillside or across open fields on a clear night can be amazing.

Moon bathing

Moon bathing is like sunbathing; you just do it under the moon instead! People have been doing this for centuries and believe it can help you feel calm and refreshed. Why not try it by taking a blanket out with you on your walk and spending a little time just lying under the moon, paying attention to how it makes you feel?

What moon phase can you see?

The moon is amazing – did you know it has no light of its own, it is just reflecting the light of the sun?

The moon is actually four hundred times smaller than the sun but it looks about the same size because it is much closer to Earth.

If you watch the moon regularly you will see how it appears to change shape throughout a month.

As the moon goes around the Earth, the sun lights up different parts of it, making it look like the moon changes shape even though it doesn't actually change at all. These different shapes are called phases of the moon.

Full Moon

Waxing Gibbous

Waning Gibbous

First Quarter

Third Quarter

Waxing Crescent

Waning Crescent

35 | Make a Kite

Flying a kite is one of the most thrilling and relaxing things to do. But you don't have to go and buy a kite in order to have that experience. It is easy and fun to make your own.

You will need

- A large piece of newspaper

- Two straight sticks, one about two-thirds the length of the other

- A ball of string

- Sticky tape or glue

- A string of trailing plants to make a tail (bindweed or ivy work really well). Alternatively, you could use a ribbon.

How to make it

1. Ask your grown-up to carefully carve a small notch into both ends of each wooden stick in the same direction (for example, horizontal).

2. Next, lay out your sticks to make a cross. Place the shorter one across the longer one about four fifths of the way up. Use a piece of string to tie the sticks together where they cross.

3. Cut another long piece of string and slide it into the notches around the ends of the sticks. Pull so it feels taut, then knot it.

4. Now cut your newspaper into the shape of the kite frame but about 5 cm bigger all the way round.

5. Fold the newspaper over the kite frame, pressing the edges down on the inside and using sticky tape or glue to secure them.

6. Attach the ball of string left over to the centre of the cross.

7. Attach the tail of leaves or ribbon to the bottom of your kite.

How to fly it

Choose a dry day when there is a bit of wind, but not too much or your kite might break.

Find an open space to fly your kite, away from trees, houses or water.

Work out which way the wind is blowing and stand with your back to the wind. Holding your kite upright, throw it upwards and release it into the air as you move forwards. You will need to release the string to let your kite fly, but keep it fairly taut.

36 | Measuring walk

Nature is full of interesting things to observe and record. One way to do this is to take measurements. Measuring helps us to learn maths skills, and it can be really fun too.

Here are five different ways to measure things in nature. You could add one (or more!) into your next walk, or plan a measuring adventure where you try them all.

Measure the length of your walk

Think of a walk that you do regularly – have you ever wondered how far you walk? This is how to find out.

You will need

- A measuring tape
- Your memory skills

> An experiment is a question which science poses to Nature, and a measurement is the recording of Nature's answer.
> Max Planck

How to measure

1. Before you start your walk, you need to work out the length of one of your steps. Mark a spot on the floor then stand with your heels on that spot. Take one normal step and mark the spot on the floor where the heel of your front foot is (you may need to ask someone to help you with this). Measure the distance between these two spots to get the length of one step.

2. Head out for your walk and count your steps as you go. You don't have to measure your whole walk if it's too long – you could just do your street, for example.

3. Make a note of the number of steps you took on your walk, or try to remember it. An alternative is to track your steps on a smartphone or smartwatch.

4. When you get home, you can work out how far you walked with this sum:

number of steps x length of one step = total distance walked

5. It's fun to guess the length of your walk before you set off, then compare your estimate to the actual distance. How close were you?

Measure the depth of a puddle

This is a brilliant thing to do when it's raining!

You will need

- A stick
- Some string
- A ruler or measuring tape

How to measure

1. Find a straight stick and a muddy puddle (it needs to be on muddy ground, not on a paved path).

2. Push the stick into the mud at the centre of the puddle.

3. Tie a piece of string around the stick just above the water level.

4. Come back a bit later and, if the puddle has got bigger, tie another piece of string just above the new water level.

5. Remove the stick from the puddle and use a ruler or measuring tape to measure the distance from the bottom of the stick to each piece of string.

6. You can measure the first depth and the second depth, then work out the difference between these two measurements to see how much deeper the puddle has become.

7. You can also measure puddles when it isn't raining – when you come back to measure a second time, has any water evaporated?

Measure the height of a tree

This works really well if there is plenty of space around a tree.

You will need

- A stick
- Measuring tape

How to measure

1. Choose a tree to measure – it needs to be on level ground.

2. Find a straight stick the same length as your arm.

3. Hold the end of the stick in your hand so that it points straight up, then straighten out your arm.

4. Walk towards or away from the tree until the top of your stick lines up with the top of the tree, and the bottom of the stick lines up with the bottom of the tree.

5. The distance between you and the tree is roughly the same as the tree's height. Use your measuring tape to measure the distance from you to the tree to find out how tall it is.

Measure nature with a ruler

See how many things you can measure with just a simple ruler.

You will need

- A ruler or measuring tape
- A pencil
- Some paper
- Lots of things to measure!

How to measure

1. Great natural items to measure include leaves, sticks, rocks, flowers, feathers, seeds, puddles, footprints and spider's webs.

2. Use a ruler or measuring tape to measure your item, then record it on your paper.

3. If you use the same unit of measurement each time, you will be able to compare your results more easily. Centimetres work well.

4. You could also measure more than one of the same type of thing, for example, different-sized leaves.

5. When you get home, you could turn your results into a bar chart.

Measure rainfall

Make a simple rain gauge and use it to measure how much rain falls.

You will need

- An empty plastic bottle or glass jar
- A marker pen
- A ruler

How to measure

1. If you're using a plastic bottle, ask an adult to cut the top off.

2. Stand the ruler up next to your bottle or jar and use a marker pen to mark centimetres up the side.

3. Find somewhere outdoors to position your rain gauge. It needs to be in the open and away from anything that might catch some of the rain. Push the bottle or jar into the ground to keep it upright, but make sure you leave the top sticking out above ground.

4. Come back to your rain gauge every day and make a note of the amount of rain in there. Then empty it out and replace it.

5. Perhaps you could take a reading every day for a week, then work out the total rainfall in that week.

37 | Alphabet games

Walking creates a brilliant opportunity to play games and there are so many to pick from. Why not give them all a go and see which one you enjoy the most?

The 'name it' game

Choose any topic, such as boys' names, animals or countries, and go through the alphabet taking it in turns to think of a word that starts with each letter. For example:

A – Ajay

B – Barney

C – Cole

D – Danny

...and so on.

Everyone gets one pass (Q and Z are tough!) and if you get all the way through the alphabet, do it again using the same topic but having to come up with different answers until someone is out!

Letter observation game

Each person chooses a letter from the alphabet and, as they walk, tries to spot things that begin with their letter. Tally up how many you find and see who spots the most.

Because this can be tricky, it is fine to use descriptive words too. So, if you have chosen the letter 'B', for example, you could say...

Bush

Blue sky

Big tree

Bird

Each descriptive word can only be used once.

What's in the bag?

This is a great guessing game to play with your friends. Take a backpack on your walk and hide an object inside it. The rest of the group has to try to work out what the object is by asking you questions about it, and the only answers you can give are 'yes' or 'no'. Each person can ask ten questions, and the first person to guess the object is the winner. If you want to give your friends a clue, you could tell them which letter the object starts with.

Will they work it out or will you have to tell them? Obviously don't take anything too heavy or it will feel like a long walk!

A-Z spotting game

This game is a combination of the first two games on the previous page. You really have to keep your eyes peeled for this one! Work through the alphabet on your walk (as a group or individually), spotting things beginning with each letter of the alphabet.

You might have to be a bit creative...

C – Creepy crawly
F – Footprint
M – Massive spider's web
Z – Zzzz sleeping dog

Can you cross off every letter?

Have fun on your walks!

Have fun with these spooky Halloween games and activities. You can do them at any time in autumn too!

Halloween nature hunt

Head out for a Halloween walk and see what spooky things you can find in nature. Can you use your imagination to transform things you see and hear into something a little bit creepy?

Here are some ideas to get you started:

• Sticks can be turned into magic wands, or a broomstick.

• Leaves can become bat wings.

• Conkers look like eyes.

• Spider's webs could mean that witches are nearby (in medieval times people believed they were a witch's companion).

• Shadows could become all sorts of creatures.

• The sound of rustling leaves, birds, the wind, or snapping twigs could be turned into something spooky.

When witches go riding, and black cats are seen, the moon laughs and whispers, 'tis near Halloween.

Anonymous

Pumpkin fairy house

Leaves, twigs, acorns, berries, feathers and seed pods all make fantastic decorations for a pumpkin fairy house. Collect some next time you go for a walk, then have fun making your pumpkin house when you get home.

How to make it

1. Ask a grown-up to cut the top off your pumpkin, then scoop out all the seeds and stringy bits.

2. Decide how many doors and windows you would like your house to have, then draw an outline of them on the pumpkin. A grown-up can then cut them out for you.

3. Now it's time to decorate. Be inspired by the materials you have collected – what could you turn them into?

- Twigs are good for window frames, paths and furniture.

- Colourful autumn leaves make lovely rugs, blankets or general decorations.

- Feathers can be used for beds.

- Conkers and acorns could be seats.

4. When your pumpkin house is finished, pop an electric tealight inside and it's ready to display.

Tree boggart

A boggart is a creature from folk tales and myths. They were thought to live either in houses or in woodland. Boggarts are a bit like goblins, and they're very mischievous – so they'd definitely enjoy trick or treating!

It's lots of fun to make a boggart face on a tree trunk, using clay and other natural materials. To protect the environment, you would need to make sure the clay is natural.

You can make your boggart as simple or as detailed as you like. Could you have a contest with your friends to see who can make the scariest one?

How to make it

1. Hunt for your natural materials – think about what might work well for a boggart's face.

2. When you're ready to create your boggart, start by making a flat piece of clay for the face.

3. Press the clay onto a tree trunk.

4. Decorate the clay with your natural materials to create eyes, nose, mouth, ears and hair.

Nature skeleton

Gather some fallen twigs, leaves, stones, nuts and seeds to make a scary skeleton.

Here are some tips:
- A leaf makes a good skull.

- Twigs are great for bones. Use bigger ones for the arms and legs, and smaller ones for the hands, feet, neck and ribs.

- Conkers, acorns and stones work well as eyes.

- Seed pods, stones and small leaves can be used for hands and feet.

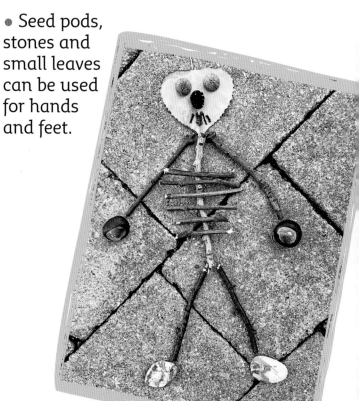

Broomsticks and wands

Sticks and twigs make excellent wands and broomsticks.

To make a broomstick, you need a large, straight stick, lots of small twigs, and some string. Use the string to tie the twigs to one end of the stick. Then you're ready to fly!

You can keep your wand simple – just a stick – or make it more fancy. Page 92 shows you how to make a wand from a stick and some leaves.

Halloween costume relay race

This game works well in a park or garden, where you have lots of room. You can play it in two teams, or compete against each other in one team by timing each player.

How to play

1. Decide on a start point and an end point.

2. Put a Halloween costume (or just some Halloween accessories like a headband, wig or witch's hat) at the end point.

3. The first player races from the start point to the end point, puts on the costume, then races back to the start, takes the costume off and gives it to the next player.

4. The next player grabs the costume and races to the end point, where they put the costume on. They then race back to the start, take the costume off and hand it to the next player.

5. Repeat step 4 until all players have had a turn.

6. The fastest team or player is the winner.

107

Humans have been tracking animals for thousands of years. Originally this was to help with hunting and staying safe, but nowadays we can use animal tracking to learn about nature and the creatures that share our environment.

Tips for tracking wildlife

You can track wildlife anywhere outdoors. Your garden, the local park, your school field or on any outdoor walk.

The most important tools for tracking are your observational skills. You need to think like a detective and look carefully for signs that animals and insects have been around. What can you see, hear, smell and touch that gives you a clue?

Safety tips

Remember, don't get too close to a wild animal, even if it seems friendly, and make sure you wash your hands thoroughly after wildlife tracking.

Things to look out for:

- **Footprints.** These are easiest to spot in mud, sand and damp ground.

- **Holes.** Some animals make their homes in burrows under the ground. Look out for small holes in the earth; there may also be a scattering of soil around the hole which the animal has dug out to make its burrow.

Some types of birds make their nests in holes in trees, so look out for those too.

- **Nests.** Birds often make their nests in trees and hedges, but you might also spy a squirrel's nest in a large tree.

If you find a nest at ground level, it could belong to a vole, hedgehog, mouse or even a bird.

It's really important that you don't touch or disturb any nests you find. They might be in use!

- **Eggshells.** An empty eggshell could mean there's a bird's nest nearby.

- **Webs.** Spiders build their webs all year round, but in autumn they are easier to spot because they are often covered in drops of water or frost.

- **Slime trails.** Slugs and snails leave a trail of slime behind them. Can you track where they went?

- **Cocoons and chrysalises.** Caterpillars form cocoons (moths) and chrysalises (butterflies) before they transform, so you could see these attached to plants, fences or trees.

- **Poo.** Animal droppings are a big clue that there's wildlife about. You should only ever observe animal poo – don't touch it as it may contain some nasty bacteria.

- **Damage to trees or bushes.** Larger animals might have flattened grass or plants, or rubbed up against trees and damaged their bark. Some animals scratch tree trunks too.

- **Feathers.** Birds naturally lose feathers in late summer, so you may see them lying on the ground in autumn. Can you work out which bird the feather came from?

- **Fur.** Animals may have shed some of their fur, or left some on fences they have brushed against.

- **Signs of feeding.** A pile of nutshells, stripped pine cones, nibbled apples, or berry seeds are all sure signs that there is wildlife close by.

Things to think about while tracking:

As you start to build up your clues, you can try to work out what they might mean. Here are some questions to get you started:

- What type of wildlife left these tracks? If you're not sure, you could take a photo, or sketch your finding and look it up later.

- What was the creature doing here? Was it looking for food, building shelter, caring for young, just passing through or something else?

- What time of day do you think it was here? Why?

- Where do you think it went after?

- Are there any other signs that might be connected to this one? Can you build up a picture of the creature's activity?

Winter

In winter the plants and trees stop growing and many animals scurry away to hibernate. The sun doesn't shine for so long each day and it might feel chilly. Perhaps you think it is time to get cosy indoors?

No! Pull on your warmest clothes and head outside. Winter is the most excellent time to get out and about as nature is fascinating at this time of year and there is so much to do!

You could learn to make your own frost or head out with a magnifying glass on a frosty walk. You could make a compass, learn to map read or hide painted stones around your neighbourhood. Maybe you would like to go geocaching or decorate a solstice tree?

Games keep you warm on a winter walk, and we have some brilliant ones for you try out as well as a winter-themed scavenger hunt and puzzle page. We also have lots of nature-based random acts of kindness for you to take part in.

There are so many great reasons to get outside over the winter season.

Wrap up warm and let's go...

40 | Winter nature challenges

At this time of year, it's tempting to snuggle up indoors and spend less time playing outside. But spending time outside in daylight can help us to feel happier, stay healthy and even live longer – so it's really important to keep going outside!

These nature challenges will keep you busy – and warm – when you're going for a walk or playing outdoors.

You will need

- A stopwatch (there might be one on your watch, or you could ask a grown-up to use the stopwatch on their smartphone)

- A paper cup

There are two ways to do these challenges:

1. If you are doing them on your own: time yourself doing each challenge, then do it again to see if you can beat your time or measurement.

2. If you are doing them with someone else: take turns doing each challenge, trying to beat each other's time or measurement.

You can pick and choose your challenges based on where you are or simply which ones sound like the most fun.

For each challenge, make sure you decide on a 'base' before you start.

The challenges

1. Find five stones, then bring them back to base and use them to build a tower that doesn't fall over.

2. Choose a marker, for example, a tree. Balance your paper cup on your head and walk to the marker, then back to base, without the cup falling off your head.

3. Find some twigs, then bring them back to base and use them to write the first letter of your name (or your whole name if you want a bigger challenge).

4. Hop to the nearest tree, then run back to base.

5. Collect three different-shaped leaves in your paper cup and bring them back to base.

6. Make an obstacle course using things you find in nature, then have a go at it.

7. Set a timer for 2 minutes and find the longest stick you can in this time.

8. Create a long jump. Use sticks or stones to mark the start point and the length of your jumps.

9. Set a timer for 1 minute. See how many different fallen nature treasures you can fill your paper cup with in this time.

10. Make up your own nature challenge – what can you find to inspire you?

41 | Nature gratitude scavenger hunt

The end of the year is a lovely time to think about all the good things we have in our lives. Doing this can help you feel positive, and by showing gratitude to the people and things that make you happy, you can spread that positivity far and wide.

Nature is absolutely full of things that make our lives happier and better. This scavenger hunt is all about being thankful for everything that nature gives us.

Give it a go when you're next out on a walk – and remember you don't have to do it all at once. Spreading it out over a few weeks is actually a brilliant way to get into the habit of seeing the good in things every day.

> Gratitude is happiness doubled by wonder.
> G. K. Chesterton

114

You can choose anything from nature for each idea on the list – so you can do it more than once as well!

1. Something with a texture that you like ☐

2. Something that would make a friend happy ☐

3. Something that helps local wildlife ☐

4. Something in your favourite colour ☐

5. Something that improves your local area ☐

6. Something that benefits the planet ☐

7. Something that could be a gift for someone special ☐

8. Something with a nice sound ☐

9. Something that makes you smile ☐

10. Something you can use in a way that it wasn't originally made for ☐

11. Something with a lovely smell ☐

12. Something in nature that makes you feel peaceful ☐

You can also do this activity every season, then compare your lists. It's really interesting to see what you notice at different times of the year.

42 | Find your way with a compass

Did you know that Earth is like a giant magnet that has its own magnetic field? The north end of a compass is drawn to Earth's magnetic North Pole and that's why we can use it to give us directions on our walks.

People in China learned how to make magnetic compasses more than 10,000 years ago. They found that when magnetised bits of iron floated in water, they would always point to magnetic north. This was incredibly helpful and led to the creation of compasses to help sailors find their way whilst at sea.

Compasses have a magnetised needle that spins freely. The needle keeps spinning until it stops at magnetic north. A compass will also show you where east, south and west are, so once you are facing north, you can find your way no matter where you might want to go.

Walking with a compass is great fun, so why not have a go at making your own?

You will need

- A bowl
- Some water
- A plastic bottle cap
- A paperclip
- A magnet

How to make it

1. Fill the bowl with water.

2. Float the bottle cap in the bowl of water.

3. Take your paperclip and carefully straighten it out.

4. Magnetise the straightened-out paperclip by stroking it with the magnet about thirty to forty times. Only stroke it in one direction and make sure you pull the magnet away from the paperclip each time you reach the end, before returning it to the start point again.

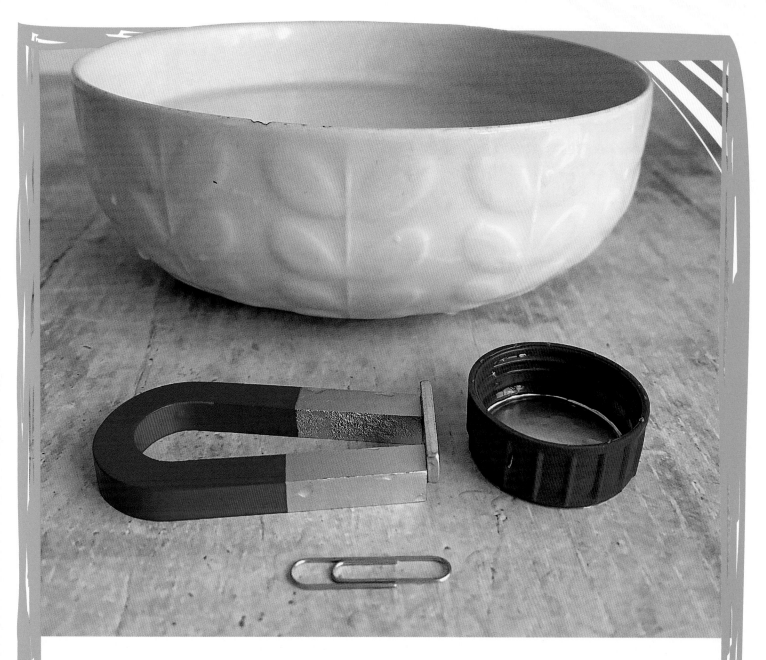

5. Lay the paperclip across the very centre of the bottle cap.

6. The paperclip should slowly turn the bottle cap until it points to magnetic north. Use another compass or a compass app on a smartphone to work out which end of the paperclip is pointing north.

7. If the paperclip does not rotate and find north, try running the magnet across it a few more times, in the same direction as before, to make sure it is properly magnetised.

This may take a few attempts but don't give up – when it works it is super exciting!

Treasure hunting with a compass

Now you know how to make a compass, it is time to have a go at using one, so let's go treasure hunting!

You will need

- A portable compass (either an app or a physical compass)

- Treasure (this could be anything, but make it something easy to spot)

To set up a treasure hunt, simply hide your treasure in your garden or local park and create a list of instructions to find it, using compass bearings.

Using a compass might seem complicated to start with, but it is pretty easy. Remember the needle will **always** search for north. Once it has found it you can see where east, south and west are and begin to plot your route.

How to write the instructions

1. Decide on your starting point.

2. Take an interesting route to get to where you hid the treasure, and, using your compass, write down the directions. They might look something like this:

   a Take 20 steps north.

   b Take 15 steps west.

   c Take 15 steps south.

   d Take 30 steps east.

3. Now give your directions to someone else and challenge them to find the treasure you have hidden!

Using the sun to find your way

Another natural way to find which direction you are facing is to look at a sunrise and sunset.

When you face a sunrise, you are facing east; west is behind you, north will be on your left and south will be on your right.

When you face a sunset, you are facing west; east is behind you, north is on your right and south on your left.

43 | Nature decorations for winter solstice

Winter solstice is the shortest day of the year, which is usually 21 or 22 December.

A lovely way you can celebrate winter solstice is to decorate an outdoor tree or bush with nature ornaments. As well as having fun and creating something beautiful, you can also help local wildlife with some edible decorations.

Here are some ideas for natural decorations – you can of course come up with your own ideas too. Just make sure that everything you use is from nature and safe for wildlife.

Ice ornament

You will need

- Nature treasures

- A shallow tray, or a plastic lid from an ice-cream or margarine tub

- A skewer or knitting needle

- Some string

How to make it

1. Place your tray or lid on a flat surface and pour water in until it's almost full.

2. Arrange your nature treasures in the water.

3. Carefully place the tray or lid in the freezer.

4. When the water has frozen, take the tray or lid out of the freezer and remove the ice.

5. Ask a grown-up to make a hole near the top of your ice ornament using a skewer or knitting needle. This is easier to do if you pop the skewer or knitting needle in some warm water first.

6. Thread some string through the hole to make a hanging loop.

7. Hang your ice ornament outdoors.

Stick snowflake

You might like to make a few of these in different sizes.

You will need

- Sticks or twigs
- Some string

How to make it

1. Start with three sticks that are roughly the same length. If your sticks are different lengths, you can snap them to make them the same size.

2. Arrange the sticks so that they cross over each other in the middle and make a six-pointed snowflake shape.

3. Use a length of string to tie the sticks together in the middle. Wrap the string around each stick a few times to make it secure, then tie a knot. It helps to have an extra pair of hands to hold the sticks while you tie them.

4. Tie another length of string to the end of one of the sticks to make a hanging loop.

5. Hang up your stick snowflake.

Orange peel garland

This is a fun way to make a gorgeous natural decoration. You could also hang it on an indoor plant.

You will need

- An orange
- A chopping board
- Small cookie cutters
- A blunt darning needle
- Some string

How to make it

1. Carefully remove the peel from your orange – try to keep it in large pieces. It helps to make a cut in the peel from the top of the orange to the bottom; you can ask a grown-up to do this for you.

2. Place the peel orange-side down on the chopping board and use a cookie cutter to stamp out shapes.

3. Use the darning needle to make a hole in each stamped-out shape.

4. Decide how long you want your garland to be, then cut a piece of string which is slightly longer than this length.

5. Tie one end of the string into a hanging loop.

6. Thread the other end of the string through the darning needle.

7. Use the needle to thread each stamped-out shape onto the string. Move each shape along the string as you go so that they are nicely spaced out.

8. When you've threaded all your shapes onto the string, remove the darning needle from the string and tie the end into another hanging loop.

9. Hang your garland in the branches of a tree or bush.

Pine cone bird feeder

If you've collected any pine cones on a nature walk this season, you can turn them into a tasty treat for local wildlife.

You will need

- Pine cones
- Solid vegetable fat or peanut butter
- Bird seed
- Some string

How to make them

1. If you're using vegetable fat, cut it into small pieces and put it in a bowl with the bird seed.

2. Use a spoon or your hands to mix everything together. This can get a bit messy!

3. Roll each pine cone in your bird seed mix so that the mix fills all the gaps and sticks to the outside. If your seed mix is a bit too soft, you can use a blunt knife or a spoon to spread it onto the pine cones.

4. If you're using peanut butter, use a blunt knife or a spoon to spread it onto the surface of the pine cones.

5. Put some bird seed on a plate and roll each pine cone in it so that the seed sticks to the peanut butter.

6. Tie a short length of string to the top of each pine cone, to make a hanging loop.

7. Hang your bird feeders in a tree.

44 | Walking games

Walks never need to be boring! With a bit of imagination, you can turn even the most familiar walk into something new and fun.

I see

1. Decide who is going to be 'it'.

2. The person who is 'it' chooses something that they can see, then says, "I see with my little eye, something beginning with (*the first letter of that word*)."

3. Everyone else takes it in turns to guess what the word is.

4. The person who guesses correctly becomes 'it' for the next round.

Walking is man's best medicine.
Hippocrates

Toss a Coin

1. Take a coin with you on the walk.

2. Every time you get to a corner, or want to change direction, toss the coin.

3. If it lands on heads, you turn left; if it lands on tails, you turn right.

4. Continue tossing the coin to choose your route. Does it take you somewhere familiar, or somewhere you've never been before?

Follow the Leader

1. Decide who is going to be the leader.

2. The leader leads the way, and everyone else follows them.

3. The leader can add in some actions while walking, which everyone else has to copy. For example, a hop, a skip, a wave, a sound or a tiptoe.

4. You can take it in turns to be the leader, or choose a leader for each different walk.

5. To make things more tricky, you can have more than one leader during the walk, with each leader adding a new action. Everyone has to do all the old actions, and add in the new one each time.

Group Counting

1. The aim is to count from 1 to 20.

2. Starting with 1, everybody joins in to call out numbers in the right order (1,2,3 and so on).

3. If two or more people say the same number at the same time, you have to start counting from 1 all over again.

4. When you manage to reach 20, the game starts again.

5. As you get better, you can make the game harder by increasing the number you count up to.

Memory Game

1. Choose a scenario for your memory game – for example, things you bought at the shop, things you have seen today.

2. One person starts by saying the scenario phrase, then an item – for example, "I went to the shop and I bought a loaf of bread."

3. The next person adds an item – for example, "I went to the shop and I bought a loaf of bread and a magazine."

4. Everyone takes it in turns to add an item to the list. They must remember and say everything on the list each time. As the list gets longer, the game gets harder!

5. When someone forgets an item on the list, the game ends and you can start a new one.

45 | Nature puzzles

On a cold winter's day, what's more fun than a puzzle that takes you outside (in your mind at least!). Answers are at the bottom of the page.

Nature jumble
Rearrange the jumbled letters to find nature words.

loucdy	gohedgeh
karp	desrpi
ssrag	tan
gerdab	alef
ticks	rryeb

Nature riddle time
What has a bed but never sleeps?

I fly without wings; I cry without eyes. What am I?

What does a tree do when it is ready to go home?

Which animal can jump higher than a tree?

What kind of tree can you carry in your hand?

Puzzling Puns
How does a sunflower whistle?

What season is best for trampolining?

What goes up when the rain comes down?

Which side of a tree has the most leaves?

What is the cutest season?

Puzzling Puns answers:-
Through its tulips, Spring!
An umbrella, The outside,
Aww-tumn

Nature riddle time answers:-
A river, A cloud, It leaves,
All of them - trees can't jump,
A palm tree

Nature jumble answers:-
cloudy, park, grass, badger, stick,
hedgehog, spider, ant, flea, berry

"Dare to ask questions and seek answers to the puzzles of life."
Lailah Gifty Akita

127

46 | Making frost

If you go for a walk on a cold day, you might spot frost on the ground, on trees and plants, or even on spider's webs. But have you ever wondered how and why frost forms?

This simple science experiment is a fun way to study frost, and if you like, you can get creative and turn your results into a frosty decoration.

You will need

- An empty, clean metal can
- Ice cubes
- A sandwich bag
- A rolling pin
- A spoon
- Some salt

How to make it

Be careful! The rim of the can could be sharp, so make sure you don't put your fingers anywhere near it.

1. Ask a grown-up to help you crush the ice. Put some ice cubes into a sandwich bag, then use the rolling pin to bash them until they break up into small pieces.

2. Use the spoon to fill the can with crushed ice. Stop when it's almost full.

3. Sprinkle salt on top of the crushed ice.

4. Watch the outside of the can – what happens?

What's going on?

When air cools, water vapour in the air turns into dew, or water droplets. Adding salt lowers the freezing point of water and forces the ice in the can to melt (a reaction that absorbs heat from the surrounding environment).

When the surface of the can falls below freezing point, it cools the area around the can and makes the water vapour in the air freeze to the surface, forming frost.

47 | Map reading

Many people simply use a sat nav in their car or look up maps on their phone when they want directions. But printed maps can also be very useful, especially when you're out walking, sailing or camping, or when you want to plan the best route.

Reading a map might seem difficult to start with, but it can be a lot of fun and it is easier than it looks. A map is really just a piece of paper filled with lines and symbols that tell you where things are in relation to each other. A map can be great for helping you to discover an area and some of the interesting things that are there.

A map reading challenge

First look at a map of the world.
1. Can you find the country you live in?

2. Can you find any other countries you might have visited or have family living in?

> *There are those who follow maps, and those who make them.*
> Alberto Villoldo

Now look at a map of your country.
1. Can you see which area you live in?

2. Can you find one other area on your country map which you have visited?

Finally, take a look at a map of the village, town or city you live in.
1. Can you find out the symbols for the following (there is usually a legend or key somewhere on the map):

- A road
- A footpath
- A river or stream
- A school
- A wooded area

2. Can you find your home?

3. Can you trace with your finger how to get from your home to your school?

4. Can you see the route to your local park?

Now that you have figured out how map reading works and how simple it is, it's time to try making a map of your own.

Making your map

Your map, like every map, needs to contain these four things:

Title – The title lets you know exactly what the map is showing, such as 'My Neighbourhood' or 'My Local Park'.

Scale – The scale gives you the ratio of a distance on a map to the distance in the real world. For example, 10 cm on the map could represent 1 km in the real world.

Legend – A map legend (or key to symbols) lists all the symbols used on a map and shows what they represent. For example, a cross on the map could be used to show where a church is, or a wiggly blue line could be a river.

Compass – The map compass is there to show the directions north, south, east and west. Some maps just have a single arrow pointing northwards. North is nearly always at the top of a map.

Decide which area you want to make a map of, then have a go.

Happy mapmaking!

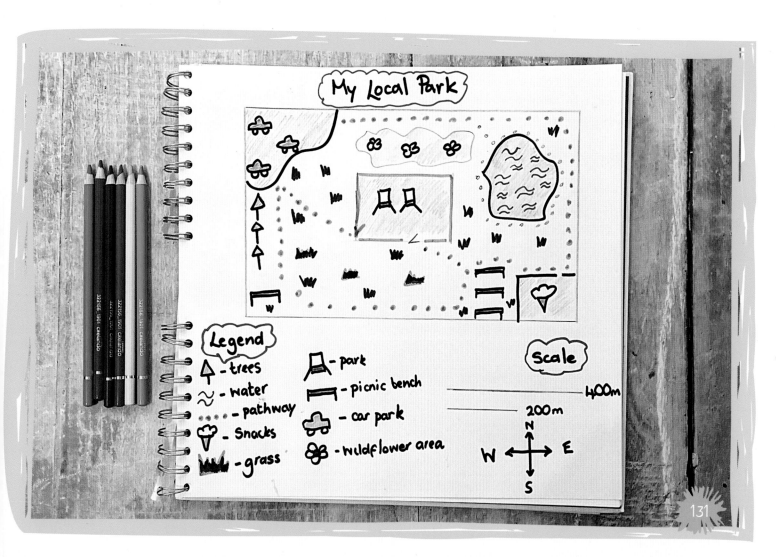

48 | Hide a painted stone walk

Doing something nice for your local community is a fantastic way to make the people who live there feel good. This painted stone project will help to put a smile on someone's face, and it's also perfect for making a walk more interesting.

This activity began in America in 2015 and is called the Kindness Rocks Project. The idea is to decorate a stone with a design of your choice, then hide it somewhere in your local area so that someone else can find it and enjoy it. The person who finds your stone can then hide it again for someone else to find.

The lovely thing about this activity is that one little act of kindness can end up bringing happiness to lots of people. Isn't that amazing?

You will need

- Clean, dry stones (smooth pebbles are best)

- Acrylic paint or poster paint

- A paintbrush

- Mod Podge or varnish

How to paint them

1. Paint your design on the top surface of a stone.

2. You might like to add a message as well, to encourage people to hide your stone again.

3. When the paint is dry, apply a layer of Mod Podge or varnish to your stone to seal it.

4. When the sealant is dry, you're ready to hide your stone.

Things to think about when hiding your stones

- Where is a good place to hide your stones? Think about how easy it will be to find them.

- Do you want to hide all of your stones on the ground, or put some higher up on a bench or wall?

- Are you going to hide all of your stones on one walk, or take one with you to hide every time you go out?

- Make sure you stay safe when hiding your stones. Don't step into roads, and only hide them on public land.

Variations

- You could make a collection of stones on a theme – for example, a hobby you enjoy, stone pets, or flags of the world.

- You could make a special set of painted stones for specific events in the year – for example, Christmas, Valentine's Day or Easter.

- Perhaps your school might like to get involved, with all pupils making a stone for a really big community stone hunt.

133

49 | Looking closer

Nature is amazing, and when you look super close at it, you get to see all kinds of wonderful things you may not have noticed before. All you need to take on your next walk is a magnifying glass.

How to use a magnifying glass
A magnifying glass is simply a convex lens (one that bulges outwards in the centre) in a holder. It is like a basic telescope. When you look at objects through it, they look bigger. This allows you to see the detail more clearly.

When you look at an object through a magnifying glass, you need to get the magnifying glass at just the right distance between your eye and the object in order to be able to focus on it. Experiment with moving the glass nearer the object and then further away till you get it just right.

How it works
A magnifying glass makes objects appear larger because the convex (bulging) lens in the glass bends the light rays that are bouncing off the object, causing them to come together when they reach your eye. This tricks your brain into 'seeing' the object as larger than it actually is.

What to magnify on your walk
Here is a list of things that look fascinating close up, which you might want to check out:

• Tree bark	• Frost-edged leaves
• Insects	• Spider's webs
• Dew on grass	• Snowflakes
• Pebbles	• Seeds
• Shells	• Soil
• Buds	• Bulbs

Plus anything else you can think of!

Make a viewfinder

Another way to look more closely at something is to focus on it intently. A viewfinder can help with this. A viewfinder is simply a square that you can look through to help you concentrate on just one view or object, and not get distracted by what else is around it.

You can make a super simple viewfinder out of four sticks, each about 5 cm long, tied at the corners with string to make a square.

Try looking at a variety of different things through your viewfinder, such as frosty grass, ducks on the river, tree branches or a pigeon. You might be so fascinated by what you see that you come home and draw a picture of it or write a piece of poetry or story about it.

Looking closely at anything helps you see it so much more clearly!

Top tip

If you don't have string or sticks to hand, try making a viewfinder out of your thumbs and index fingers formed into a rectangle.

50 | Random acts of nature Kindness

Random Acts of Kindness Day takes place each year on 17 February all across the world. It is a day when people are encouraged to perform small acts of kindness to make the world a better and brighter place.

Acts of kindness could and should be done every day but on this special day it's good to go the extra mile and really focus on, and celebrate, kindness. Being kind to yourself and to other people is very important but we MUST also remember that the planet needs our kindness too.

Lots of things in nature – including animals, insects and plants – are struggling due to climate change, loss of habitat or pollution. Nature needs our help, and there are many small acts of kindness that we can show it.

See how many of these acts of kindness you can complete on your walks this week.

The world is full of Kind people. If you can't find one, be one.
Nishan Panwar

Begin a pet food collection at school for your local animal shelter

Plant something

Have a no screen day, save electricity, and play games outside instead

Make a heart from twigs and leave it on a path to make a stranger smile

Visit your local library (the same books are reused there again and again!)

Offer to help an elderly neighbour sweep leaves/ shovel snow

Hunt the house for old blankets and donate them to an animal rescue centre

Make a bug hotel out of sticks

Feed the ducks with seed (not bread, which isn't healthy for them)

Pick up someone else's litter

Hug a tree and promise to protect it

Use both sides of the paper you are drawing on – save the trees!

Leave a dish of water out for birds to drink from

Make something from rubbish that can't be recycled, to stop it going into landfill

Walk or cycle instead of using a car

Send a packet of wildflower seeds to a friend with a note saying how much you care about them

Make a picture out of fallen bits of nature to give to someone you love

Donate your pocket money to your local wildlife trust (or another nature charity)

Make, rather than buy, a thank you card and send it to a coach or teacher you admire

Upcycle something and give it a new life (you could turn an old tyre or welly into a planter for the garden)

51 | Geocaching

Geocaching (pronounced *geo-cash-ing*) is a brilliant way to explore the world around you with your family and friends. It is kind of like a treasure hunt and it really tests your observational skills. It doesn't matter where you are, there's probably treasure somewhere nearby!

You will need

- A smartphone
- The Geocaching® app
- A pen

How it works

First, ask your grown-up to download the Geocaching® app onto a smartphone. Then you simply follow the directions to find your way to hidden containers called 'geocaches'.

Latitude and longitude provide the cache's location and you will be given the correct coordinates to follow. This takes a bit of practice at first but you will soon get the hang of it. Other geocachers who have previously found the cache might also have left clues online.

Some geocaches are easy to find and some will be more tricky – you will have to keep your eyes wide open, and search high and low.

Some caches may contain a small item (which you can take and replace with one of your own) or they may just contain a logbook for you to sign and replace.

Did you know...?
There are millions of geocaches in 190 countries around the world, all just waiting to be discovered – there are probably some right near you and you don't even know it (yet!).

Geocaching is fun to do on holiday, in cities, towns and in the countryside or if you're out and about in your local area. It is a great reason to get outdoors and go exploring!

Treasure comes in many forms.
S. A. Rodriguez

52 | Nature rubbings walk

There are lots of fantastic textures and patterns in nature. Once you start noticing them, you will see them everywhere. You can make a record of the patterns and textures you spot by taking nature rubbings.

Next time you go for a walk, pop some paper and crayons in your bag. When you see something with an interesting texture or pattern, you're ready to be a nature artist.

You can take a rubbing of anything you like, but some things work better than others. Experiment and see what works well for you, but avoid anything that's wet as you will probably just end up with soggy, torn paper.

Here are some ideas for things that make good nature rubbings:

- Tree bark
- A tree stump
- A fallen log
- Dry leaves
- A wooden bench
- Small twigs
- A stone path
- Flat stones

You will need

- Sheets of white paper
- Wax crayons

How to do it

1. Place a sheet of paper over the item you want to take a rubbing of.

2. Hold the crayon in the hand you write with, and use your other hand to hold the paper steady.

3. Gently rub the side of the crayon over the surface of the paper. You might need to experiment with the angle of the crayon before you get it right.

4. You will see the outline of the pattern appear as darker crayon on the paper. If the pattern isn't very clear, try pressing down a bit harder with your crayon.

5. When you have finished, remove the paper.

Once you've finished your nature rubbings, think about how you could use or display them. For example, you could cut them out and make a garland, turn them into greetings cards, or make a bookmark.

Variations

You can also collect some fallen nature treasures on your walk, then make a nature rubbing or a collage when you get home. To do this, arrange your nature treasures on a piece of paper, then place another piece of paper over the top and make your rubbing with a crayon.

Perhaps you could use more than one colour, arrange your treasures in a particular pattern, or make a rubbing with a theme, such as leaves, feathers or twigs.

Index